R.U.R.

(Rossum's Universal Robots)

R.U.R.

(Rossum's Universal Robots)

KAREL ČAPEK

Translation by David Wyllie

WILDSIDE PRESS

Published by Wildside Press LLC.
www.wildsidebooks.com

DRAMATIS PERSONAE

Harry Domin: Director General, Rossum's Universal Robots
Fabry: Technical Director, R.U.R.
Dr. Gall: Head of Physiology and Research Department, R.U.R.
Dr. Hallemeier: Head of Institute for Robot Psychology and Behaviour, R.U.R
Busman: Commercial Director, R.U.R.
Alquist: Head of Construction, R.U.R.
Helena Glory
Nana: Her Nanny
Marius: Robot
Sulla: Robot, female
Radius: Robot
Damon: Robot
1st Robot
2nd Robot
3rd Robot
4th Robot
Primus: Robot
Helena: Robot, female

Robot servant
and numerous robots

Domin: in introductory scene, about thirty-eight years old, tall, clean shaven
Fabry: also clean shaven, fair, serious and delicate features
Dr. Gall: light build, lively, dark complexion and black moustache
Hallemeier: heavy build, noisy, big ginger moustache and ginger shock of hair
Busman: fat, bald, short-sighted Jew
Alquist: older than the others, dressed without care, long grey hair and beard
Helena: very elegant

In the play proper, all ten years older.

In the introductory scene, the robots are dressed like people. They are slightly mechanical in their speech and movements, blank of expression, fixed in their gaze. In the play proper they wear linen blouses seized at the waist with a belt and on their breasts wear a brass number

Intervals after the introductory scene and the second act.

INTRODUCTORY SCENE

Central office at the factory of Rossum's Universal Robots. Entrance stage right. Through the windows can be seen endless rows of factory buildings. Stage left, further administrative areas.

Domin: (*Sitting at a large American desk in a swivelling chair. On the table are a lamp, telephone, paperweight, files, letters, papers etc. On the wall, stage left, are large maps showing shipping lines and railway lines, large calendar, clock showing just before midday; on the wall stage right are printed posters: "The Cheapest Workforce You Can Get: Rossum's Robots", "Latest invention; Robots for the Tropics. 150 d. each", "Everyone Should have a Robot!", "Reduce the Cost of your Products! Order a Robot from Rossum's!". Also other maps, shipping timetable, notice board with telegrams, rates of exchange etc. In contrast with the content of the walls, the floor is covered with a magnificent Turkish carpet, stage right is as round armchair, settee, sumptuous leather armchair, bookshelves containing not books but bottles of wines and spirits. Stage left, safe. Beside Domin's desk a typewriter at which Sulla is writing*)

Domin: (*dictating*) "…cannot take responsibility for items damaged in transit. The captain of your vessel was given warning at time of loading that it was not suitable for the carriage of robots, and so damage to its cargo cannot be charged to our account. Yours faithfully, Rossum's Universal Robots." Is that it now?

Sulla: Yes.

Domin: New letter. Friedrichswerke, Hamburg. Date. "We are pleased to confirm receipt of your order for fifteen thousand robots…" (*telephone rings. Domin lifts receiver and speaks*) Hello, central office… yes…certainly…oh yes, as always…of course, send him a telegram… fine! (*hangs up*) Where were we?

Sulla: …your order for fifteen thousand robots.

Domin: (*thoughtfully*) fifteen thousand robots, fifteen thousand robots,

Marius: (*enters*) Mr. Domin, there is a lady outside who is asking…

Domin: Who is it?

Marius: I do not know. (*gives him visiting card*)

Domin: (*reading*) Mr. Glory, managing director of… Show him in!

Marius: (*opens door*) Please come in, madam.

(*enter Helena Glory. Exit Marius*)

Domin: (*standing*) Do come in.

Helena: Mr. Domin, the managing director?

Domin: At your service.

Helena: I've come to see you…

Domin: …with the visiting card of Mr. Glory — no more need be said.

Helena: Mr. Glory is my father. I'm Helena Glory.

Domin: Miss Glory, this is an exceptional honour for us that…

Helena: …that you can't just show me the door

Domin: …that we can welcome the daughter of an illustrious businessman like you father. Please take a seat. Sulla, you can go now (*exit Sulla*)

Domin: (*sitting*) How can I help you, Miss Glory?

Helena: I've come here…

Domin: …to see our factory for making people for yourself. All our visitors want to see the factory. And of course you're very welcome.

Helena: I thought it wasn't allowed to…

Domin: …enter the factory? Well, of course it's not, but everyone who comes here has a recommendation from somebody, Miss Glory.

Helena: And do you let everyone see it…?

Domin: Not all of it. Making artificial people is an industrial secret.

Helena: Why will you never let me finish what I say?

Domin: Oh, I'm sorry. Is that not what you were going to say?

Helena: I was going to ask…

Domin: …whether I might show you something in our factory that the others aren't allowed to see. Well, I'm sure that'll be OK, Miss Glory.

Helena: What makes you think that's what I was going to ask?

Domin: Everyone asks for the same thing. (*standing*) I can personally show you more than the others are allowed to see.

Helena: Thank you.

Domin: All I ask is that you don't say anything at all to anyone else.

Helena: (*stands and offers her hand*) Word of honour.

Domin: Thank you. Would you not like to take off your veil?

Helena: Oh, of course, you'll be wanting to see my face. Do excuse me.

Domin: That's all right.

Helena: And, if you would just let go of my hand...

Domin: (*releases hand*) I'm sorry, I forgot.

Helena: (*removes veil*) Do you want to make sure I'm not a spy. You seem very careful.

Domin: (*looks at her, enchanted*) Hm — oh, yes, — well — that's just how we are.

Helena: Don't you trust me?

Domin: Exceptionally. Miss, er, do excuse me Miss Glory. This really is an exceptional pleasure. Did you have a good crossing?

Helena: Yes. Why?

Domin: Because — well, that is — because you are very young.

Helena: Are we going into the factory now?

Domin: Yes. I suppose about twenty-two?

Helena: Twenty-two what?

Domin: Years.

Helena: Twenty-one. Why do you want to know that?

Domin: Because...sort of...(*with enthusiasm*) You will be staying here for some time, won't you.

Helena: That depends on how much you choose to show me.

Domin: Ah, the damned factory! But of course, Miss Glory, you can see everything. Do please sit down. Would you be interested in hearing the history of our invention?

Helena: Yes, I would. (*sits*)

Domin: Well this is what happened. (*sits at desk, seems captivated by Helena and speaks quickly*) It was in 1920 when old Rossum, still a young man then but a great scientist, came to live on this isolated island in order to study marine biology. Stop. Alongside his studies, he made several attempts to synthesise the chemical structure of living tissues, known as protoplasm, and he eventually discovered a material that behaved just the same as living tissue despite being, chemically, quite different. That was in 1932, exactly four hundred and forty years after the discovery of America.

Helena: Do you know all this by heart?

Domin: I do. Physiology really isn't my subject. Shall I carry on?

Helena: If you like.

Domin: (*triumphant*) And then, Miss Glory, this is what he wrote down in his chemical notes: "Nature has found only one way of organising living matter. There is however another way which is simpler, easier to mould, and quicker to produce than Nature ever stumbled across. This other path along which life might have developed is what I have just discovered." Just think: he wrote these words about a blob of some kind of coloidal jelly that not even a dog would eat. Imagine him sitting with a test tube and thinking about how it could grow out into an entire tree of life made of all the animals starting with a tiny coil of life and ending with…ending with man himself. Man made of different material than we are. Miss Glory, this was one of the great moments of history.

Helena: What happened next?

Domin: Next? Next he had to get this life out of the test tube and speed up its development so that it would create some of organs needed such as bone and nerves and all sorts of things and find materials such as catalysts and enzymes and hormones and so on and in short…are you understanding all of this?

Helena: I… I'm not sure. Perhaps not all of it.

Domin: I don't understand any of it. It's just that using this slime he could make whatever he wanted. He could have made a Medusa with the brain of Socrates or a worm fifty meters long. But old Rossum didn't have a trace of humour about him, so he got it into his head to make a normal vertebrate, such as human being. And so that's what he started doing.

Helena: What exactly was it he tried to do?

Domin: Imitating Nature. First he tried to make an artificial dog. It took him years and years, and the result was something like a malformed deer which died after a few days. I can show you it in the museum. And then he set to work making a human being.

(*Pause*)

Helena: And that's what I'm not allowed to tell anyone?

Domin: No-one whatsoever.

Helena: Pity it's in all the papers then.

Domin: That is a pity. (*jumps off desk and sits beside Helena*) But do you know what's not in all the papers? (*taps his forehead*) That old Rossum was completely mad. Seriously. But keep that to yourself. He was quite mad. He seriously wanted to make a human being.

Helena: Well that's what you do, isn't it?

Domin: Something like that, yes, but old Rossum meant it entirely literally. He wanted, in some scientific way, to take the place of God. He was a convinced materialist, and that's why he wanted to do everything simply to prove that there was no God needed. That's how he had had the idea of making a human being, just like you or me down to the smallest hair. Do you know anything about anatomy, Miss Glory?

Helena: Er, not really, no.

Domin: No, nor do I. But just think of how old Rossum got it into his head to make everything, every gland, every organ, just as they are in the human body. The Appendix. The tonsils. The belly-button. Even the things with no function and even, er, even the sexual organs.

Helena: But the sexual organs would, er, they'd...

Domin: They do have a function, I realise that. But if people are going to be made artificially then, er, then there's not really much need for them.

Helena: I see what you mean.

Domin: In the museum I'll show you the monstrosity he created over the ten years he was working. It was supposed to be a man, but it lived for a total of three days. Old Rossum had no taste whatsoever. This thing is horrible, just horrible what he did. But on the inside it's got all the things that a man's supposed to have. Really! The detail of the work is quite amazing. And then Rossum's nephew came out here. Now this man, Miss Glory, he was a genius. As soon as he saw what the old man was doing he said, 'This is ridiculous, to spend ten years making a man; if you can't do it quicker than Nature then you might as well give up on it'. And then he began to study anatomy himself.

Helena: That's not what they say in the papers either.

Domin: (*standing*) What they say in the papers are paid advertisements and all sorts of nonsense. They say the old man invented the robots himself, for one thing. What the old man did might have been all right for a university but he had no idea at all about industrial production. He thought he'd be making real people, real Indians or real professors or real idiots. It was young Rossum who had the idea of making robots that would be a living and intelligent workforce. What they say in the papers about the two great men working together is just a fairy tale — in fact they never stopped arguing. The old atheist had no idea about industry and commerce, and the young man ended up shutting him up in his laboratory where he could play around with his great failures while he got on with the real job himself in a proper scientific way. Old Rossum literally cursed him. He carried on in his laboratory, producing two more physiological monstrosities, until one day they found him there dead. And that's the whole story.

Helena: And then, what did the young one do?

Domin: Ah now, young Rossum; that was the start of a new age. After the age of research came the age of production. He took a good look at the human body and he saw straight away that it was much too complicated, any good engineer would design it much more simply. So he began to re-design the whole anatomy, seeing what he could leave out or simplify. In short, Miss Glory... I'm not boring you, am I?

Helena: No, quite the opposite, this is fascinating.

Domin: So young Rossum said to himself: Man is a being that does things such as feeling happiness, plays the violin, likes to go for a walk, and all sorts of other things which are simply not needed.

Helena: Oh, I see!

Domin: No, wait. Which are simply not needed for activities such as weaving or calculating. A petrol engine doesn't have any ornaments or tassels on it, and making an artificial worker is just like making a petrol engine. The simpler you make production the better you make the product. What sort of worker do you think is the best?

Helena: The best sort of worker? I suppose one who is honest and dedicated.

Domin: No. The best sort of worker is the cheapest worker. The one that has the least needs. What young Rossum invented was a worker with the least needs possible. He had to make him simpler. He threw out everything that wasn't of direct use in his work, that's to say, he threw out the man and put in the robot. Miss Glory, robots are not people. They are mechanically much better than we are, they have an amazing ability to understand things, but they don't have a soul. Young Rossum created something much more sophisticated than Nature ever did — technically at least!

Helena: They do say that man was created by God.

Domin: So much the worse for them. God had no idea about modern technology. Would you believe that young Rossum, when he was alive, was playing at God.

Helena: How was he doing that!

Domin: He started to make super-robots. Working giants. He tried to make them four meters tall — you wouldn't believe how those monsters kept breaking up.

Helena: Breaking up?

Domin: Yes. All of a sudden, for no reason, a leg or an arm would break. This planet just seems too small for monsters like that. So now we just make them normal size and normal proportions.

Helena: I saw my first robot in our village. They'd bought him so that…that's to say they'd employed him to…

Domin: Bought it, Miss Glory. Robots are bought and sold.

Helena: …they'd obtained him to work as a road sweeper. I watched him working . He was strange. So quiet.

Domin: Have you seen my typist?

Helena: I didn't really notice her.

Domin: (*rings*) You know, RUR, Ltd. has never really make individual robots, but we do have some that are better than others. The best ones can last up to twenty years.

Helena: And then they die, do they?

Domin: Yes, they get worn out.

(*enter Sulla*)

Domin: Sulla, let Miss Glory have a look at you.

Helena: (*stands and offers her hand*) Pleased to meet you. It must be very hard for you out here, cut off from the rest of the world.

Sulla: I do not know the rest of the world Miss Glory please sit down.

Helena: (*sits*) Where are you from?

Sulla: From here, the factory.

Helena: Oh, you were born here.

Sulla: Yes I was made here.

Helena: (*startled*) What?

Domin: (*laughing*) Sulla isn't a person, Miss Glory, she's a robot.

Helena: Oh, please forgive me…

Domin: (*puts his hand on Sulla's shoulder*) Sulla doesn't have feelings. You can examine her. Feel her face and see how we make the skin.

Helena: Oh, no, no!

Domin: It feels just the same as human skin. Sulla even has the sort of down on her face that you'd expect on a blonde. Perhaps her eyes are a bit small, but look at that hair. Turn around, Sulla.

Helena: Stop it!

Domin: Talk to our guest. We're very honoured to have her here.

Sulla: Please sit down miss. (*both sit*) Did you have a good crossing.

Helena: Er, yes, yes, very good thank you.

Sulla: It will be better not to go back on the Amelia Miss Glory. The barometer is dropping fast, and has sunk to 705. Wait here for the Pennsylvania, that is a very good and very strong ship.

Domin: How big is it?

Sulla: It is twelve thousand tonnes and can travel at twenty knots.

Domin: (*laughing*) That's enough now, Sulla, that's enough. Show us how well you speak French.

Helena: You speak French?

Sulla: I speak four languages. I can write 'Dear Sir! Monsieur! Geehrter Herr! Ctený pane!'

Helena: (*jumping up*) This is all humbug! You're all charlatans! Sulla's not a robot, she's a living girl just like I am. Sulla, you should be ashamed of yourself — why are you play-acting like this?

Sulla: I am a robot.

Helena: No, no, you're lying! Oh, I'm sorry, Sulla, I realise… I realise they force you to do it just to make their products look good. Sulla, you're a living girl just like I am — admit it.

Domin: Sorry Miss Glory. I'm afraid Sulla really is a robot.

Helena: You're lying!

Domin: (*stands erect*) What's that? — (*rings*) If you'll allow me, it seems I'll have to convince you.

(*enter Marius*)

Domin: Marius, take Sulla down to the dissection room to have her opened up. Quickly!

Helena: Where?

Domin: The dissection room. Once they've cut her open you can come down and have a look.

Helena: I'm not going there!

Domin: If you'll forgive me, you did say something about lying.

Helena: You're going to have her killed?

Domin: You don't kill a machine.

Helena: (*arms around Sulla*) Don't worry, Sulla, I won't let them take you. Do they always treat you like this? You shouldn't put up with it, do you hear, you shouldn't put up with it.

Sulla: I am a robot.

Helena: I don't care what you are. Robots are people just as good as we are. Sulla, would you really let them cut you open.

Sulla: Yes.

Helena: And aren't you afraid of dying?

Sulla: I do not understand dying, Miss Glory.

Helena: Do you know what would happen to you then?

Sulla: Yes, I would cease to move.

Helena: This is terrible!

Domin: Marius, tell the lady what you are.

Marius: Robot, Marius.

Domin: And would you take Sulla down to the dissection room?

Marius: Yes.

Domin: Would you not feel any pity for her?

Marius: I do not understand pity.

Domin: What would happen to her.

Marius: She would cease to move. She would be put on the scrap heap.

Domin: That's what death is, Marius. Are you afraid of death.

Marius: No.

Domin: There, Miss Glory, you see? Robots don't cling to life. There's no way they could do. They've got no sense of pleasure. They're less than the grass.

Helena: Oh stop it! Send them out of here, at least!

Domin: Marius, Sulla, you can go now.

(*Sulla and Marius exeunt*)

Helena: They're horrible. This is vile, what you're doing here.

Domin: What's vile about it?

Helena: I don't know. Why…why did you give her the name 'Sulla'?

Domin: Don't you like that name?

Helena: It's a man's name. Sulla was a Roman general.

Domin: Was he? We thought Marius and Sulla were lovers.

Helena: No, Marius and Sulla were generals who fought against each other in…oh I forget when.

Domin: Come over to the window. What do you see?

Helena: Bricklayers.

Domin: They're robots. All the workers here are robots. And down here; what do you see there?

Helena: Some kind of office.

Domin: That's the accounts department. And in the…

Helena: …lots of office workers.

Domin: They're all robots. All our office staff are robots. Over there there's the factory…

(*just then, factory whistles and sirens sound*)

Domin: Lunchtime. The robots don't know when they're supposed to stop working. At two o'clock I'll show you the mixers.

Helena: What mixers?

Domin: (*drily*) For mixing the dough. Each one of them can mix the material for a thousand robots at a time. Then there are the vats of liver and brain and so on. The bone factory. Then I'll show you the spinning-mill.

Helena: What spinning-mill?

Domin: Where we make the nerve fibres and the veins. And the intestine mill, where kilometers of tubing run through at a time. Then there's the assembly room where all these things are put together, it's just like making a car really. Each worker contributes just his own part of the production which automatically goes on to the next worker, then to the third and on and on. It's all fascinating to watch. After that they go to the drying room and into storage where the newly made robots work.

Helena: You mean you make them start work as soon as they're made?

Domin: Well really, it's more like working in the way a new piece of furniture works. They need to get used to the idea that they exist. There's something on the inside of them that needs to grow or something. And there are lots of new things on the inside that just aren't there until this time. You see, we need to leave a little space for natural development. And in the meantime the products go through their apprenticeship.

Helena: What does that involve?

Domin: Much the same as going to school for a person. They learn how to speak, write and do arithmetic, as they've got amazing memories. If you read a twenty-volume encyclopedia to them they could repeat it back to you word for word, but they never think of anything new for themselves. They'd make very good university lecturers. After that, they're sorted and distributed, fifteen thousand of them a day, not counting those that are defective and go back to the scrap heap...and so on and so on.

Helena: Are you cross with me?

Domin: God no! I just thought we...we might talk about something different. There's just a few of us here surrounded by hundreds of thousands of robots, and no women at all. All we ever talk about is production levels all day every day. It's as if there were some kind of curse on us.

Helena: I'm very sorry I called you...called you a liar.

(*knocking*)

Domin: Come in, lads.

(*Enter, stage left, Fabry, Dr. Gall, Dr. Hallemeier, Alquist*)

Dr. Gall: Oh, not disturbing you, are we?

Domin: Come on in. Miss Glory, this is Alquist, Fabry, Gall, Hallemeier. Mr. Glory's daughter.

Helena: (*embarrassed*) Good afternoon.

Fabry: We had no idea...

Dr. Gall: This is a great pleasure.

Alquist: It's nice to see you here, Miss Glory.

(*Enter Busman, right*)

Busman: Hello, what's going on here?

Domin: Come in, Busman. This is Busman, and this is Mr. Glory's daughter.

Helena: Pleased to meet you.

Busman: Oh, that's wonderful! Miss Glory, would you mind if we send a telegram to the newspapers to say you've come?

Helena: No, no, please don't do that!

Domin: Please, do sit down.

(*Fabry, Busman and Dr. Gall pull up armchairs*)

Fabry: Please…

Busman: After you…

Dr. Gall: Beg your pardon…

Alquist: Miss Glory, did you have a good journey?

Dr. Gall: Will you be staying here, with us, for long?

Fabry: What do you think of our factory, Miss Glory?

Hallemeier: Came over on the Amelia, did you?

Domin: Quiet, let Miss Glory speak.

Helena: (*to Domin*)What am I supposed to say to them?

Domin: (*surprised*)Whatever you like.

Helena: Should I…should I be open with them?

Domin: Of course you should.

Helena: (*hesitant, then decided*) Tell me, do you not mind the way you're treated?

Fabry: Treated by whom?

Helena: Any of these people.

(*All look at each other in bewilderment*)

Alquist: The way we're treated?

Dr. Gall: How do you mean?

Hallemeier: Oh my God!

Busman: But Miss Glory, dear me!

Helena: Do you not think you could have a better kind of existence?

Dr. Gall: That all depends, Miss Glory, what do you mean?

Helena: What I mean is…(*in an outburst*)…this is all horrible, it's vile! (*standing*) The whole of Europe is talking about what's going on here and the way you're treated. That's why I've come here, to see for myself, and I find it's a thousand times worse than anyone ever thought! How can you bear it?

Alquist: What is it you think we have to bear?

Helena: Your position here. You are people just like we are, for God's sake, just like anyone else in Europe, anyone else in the world! It's a scandal, the way you have to live, it isn't worthy of you!

Busman: My word, Miss Glory!!

Fabry: But I think there might be something in what Miss Glory says, lads. We really do live here like a camp of Indians.

Helena: Worse than Indians! May I, oh, may I call you 'brothers'?

Busman: Well, why on Earth not?

Helena: Brothers, I haven't come here on behalf of my father. I'm here on behalf of the League of Humanity. Brothers, the League of Humanity now has more than two thousand members. There are two thousand people who are standing up for you and want to help you.

Busman: Two thousand people! Dear me, that's quite a decent number, that's very nice indeed.

Fabry: I always say that old Europe hasn't had its day yet. Do you hear, lads, they haven't forgotten about us, they want to help us.

Dr. Gall: What sort of help do you have in mind? A theatre performance, perhaps?

Hallemeier: An orchestra?

Helena: More than that.

Alquist: Yourself?

Helena: Oh, never mind myself! I'll stay here for as long as it's needed.

Busman: Dear me, that is good news!

Alquist: I'll go and get the best room ready for Miss Glory then, Domin.

Domin: Wait a second, Alquist, I've a feeling Miss Glory hasn't quite finished speaking yet.

Helena: No, I haven't finished, not unless you mean to shut me up by force.

Dr. Gall: Harry, how dare you!

Helena: Thank you. I knew you'd protect me.

Domin: Excuse me, Miss Glory, but are you sure you're talking to robots?

Helena: (*taken aback*) Who else would I be talking to?

Domin: I'm afraid these gentlemen are people, just like you are. Just like the whole of Europe.

Helena: (*to the others*) You aren't robots?

Busman: (*laughing*) God forbid!

Hallemeier: The idea's disgusting!

Dr. Gall: (*laughing*) Well thank you very much!

Helena: But…but that's impossible.

Fabry: On my word of honour, Miss Glory, we are not robots.

Helena: (*to Domin*) Then why did you tell me that all your staff are robots?

Domin: All the staff are robots, but not the management. Let me introduce them: Mr. Fabry, general technical director, Rossum's Universal Robots. Doctor Gall, director of department for physiology and research. Doctor Hallemeier, director of the institute for robot behaviour and psychology. Mr. Busman, commercial director, and Mr. Alquist, our builder, head of construction at Rossum's Universal Robots.

Helena: I'm sorry gentlemen. I… I…oh, that's terrible, what have I done?

Alquist: Oh, it doesn't matter, Miss Glory, please sit down.

Helena: (*sitting*) What a stupid girl I am. Now, now you'll send me back on the next ship.

Dr. Gall: Not for the world. Why would we want to send you back?

Helena: Because now you know…you know…you know I want to destroy your business.

Domin: But there've already been hundreds of saviours and prophets here. More of them arrive with every ship; missionaries, anarchists, the Salvation Army, everything you can think of. It's astonishing just how many churches and madmen there are in the world.

Helena: And you let them talk to the robots?

Domin: Why not? We've let them all do it so far. The robots remember everything, but that's all they do. They don't even laugh at what people tell them. It's really quite incredible. If you feel like it, I can take you down to the storeroom and you can talk to the robots there.

Busman: Three hundred and forty-seven thousand.

Domin: All right then. You can lecture them on whatever you like. Read them the Bible, logarithmic tables, anything. You can even preach to them about human rights.

Helena: But I thought that...if they were just shown a little love...

Fabry: That's impossible, Miss Glory. There's nothing more different from people than a robot.

Helena: Why do you make them?

Busman: Ha haha, that's a good one! Why do we make robots!

Fabry: So that they can work for us, Miss Glory. One robot can take the place of two and a half workers. The human body is very imperfect; one day it had to be replaced with a machine that would work better.

Busman: People cost too much.

Fabry: They were very unproductive. They weren't good enough for modern technology. And besides,...besides...this is wonderful progress that... I beg your pardon.

Helena: What?

Fabry: Please forgive me, but to give birth to a machine is wonderful progress. It's more convenient and it's quicker, and everything that's quicker means progress. Nature had no notion of the modern rate of work. From a technical point of view, the whole of childhood is quite pointless. Simply a waste of time. And thirdly...

Helena: Oh, stop it!

Fabry: As you like. Can I ask you, what actually is it that your League...League of Humanity stands for?

Helena: It's meant to.... actually it's meant to protect the robots and make sure...make sure they're treated properly.

Fabry: That's not at all a bad objective. A machine should always be treated properly. In fact I agree with you completely. I never like it when things are damaged. Miss Glory, would you mind enrolling all of us as new paying members of your organisation.

Helena: No, you don't understand. We want, what we actually want is to set the robots free!

Hallemeier: To do what?

Helena: They should be treated...treated the same as people.

Hallemeier: Aha. So you mean they should have the vote! Do you think they should be paid a wage as well?

Helena: Well of course they should!

Hallemeier: We'll have to see about that. And what do you think they'd do with their wages?

Helena: They'd buy...buy the things they need...things to bring them pleasure.

Hallemeier: This all sounds very nice; only robots don't feel pleasure. And what are these things they're supposed to buy? They can be fed on pineapples, straw, anything you like; it's all the same to them, they haven't got a sense of taste. There's nothing they're interested in, Miss Glory. It's not as if anyone's ever seen a robot laugh.

Helena: Why...why...why don't you make them happier?

Hallemeier: We couldn't do that, they're only robots after all. They've got no will of their own. No passions. No hopes. No soul.

Helena: And no love and no courage?

Hallemeier: Well of course they don't feel love. Robots don't love anything, not even themselves. And courage? I'm not so sure about that; a couple of times, not very often, mind, they have shown some resistance...

Helena: What?

Hallemeier: Well, nothing in particular, just that sometimes they seem to, sort of, go silent. It's almost like some kind of epileptic fit. 'Robot cramp', we call it. Or sometimes one of them might suddenly smash whatever's in its hand, or stand still, or grind their teeth— and then they just have to go on the scrap heap. It's clearly just some technical disorder.

Domin: Some kind of fault in the production.

Helena: No, no, that's their soul!

Fabry: Do you think that grinding teeth is the beginnings of a soul?

Domin: We can solve that problem, Miss Glory. Doctor Gall is carrying out some experiments right now.

Dr. Gall: No, not quite yet, Domin, at present I'm working on nerves for feeling pain.

Helena: Nerves for feeling pain?

Dr. Gall: That's right. Robots have virtually no sense of physical pain, as young Rossum simplified the nervous system a bit too much. That turns out to have been a mistake and so we're working on pain now.

Helena: Why...why...if you don't give them a soul why do you want to give them pain?

Dr. Gall: For good industrial reasons, Miss Glory. The robots sometimes cause themselves damage because it causes them no pain; they do things such as pushing their hand into a machine, cutting off a finger or even smash their heads in. It just doesn't matter to them. But if they have pain it'll be an automatic protection against injuries.

Helena: Will they be any the happier when they can feel pain?

Dr. Gall: Quite the opposite, but it will be a technical improvement.

Helena: Why don't you create a soul for them?

Dr. Gall: That's not within our power.

Fabry: That wouldn't be in our interest.

Busman: That would raise production costs. Just think how cheaply we make them; a hundred and twenty dollars each, complete with clothing, and fifteen years ago they cost ten thousand! Five years ago we still had to buy the clothes for them, but now we have our own weaving mills and even sell material at a fifth of the price of other mills. Tell me, Miss Glory, what is it you pay for a metre of cloth?

Helena: I don't know... I really don't know... I've forgotten.

Busman: Dear dear me, and you were wanting to establish the League of Humanity! Cloth nowadays is three times cheaper, miss, the prices of everything are three times cheaper and they're still going down and down and down.

Helena: I don't see what you mean.

Busman: Dear lady, what I mean is that the price of labour is getting cheaper! Even with its food, a robot costs no more than three quarters of a cent per hour! It's wonderful; every factory is buying robots as quick as they can to reduce production costs, and those that aren't are going bankrupt.

Helena: Yes, that's right, and throwing their workers out on the streets.

Busman: Ha ha, well of course they are! And while they are doing that we are putting five hundred thousand tropical robots out on the Argentine pampas to cultivate wheat. Tell me, what does a loaf of bread cost where you come from?

Helena: I've no idea.

Busman: There, you see; in good old Europe, a loaf of bread now costs two cents; but that bread comes from us, do you see? Two cents a loaf; and the League of Humanity has no idea! Ha ha, Miss Glory, you do not even know if you are paying too much for a crust. Or too much for society or for anything else. But in five years' time, dear me, do sit down!

Helena: What?

Busman: In five years' time, the price will be a tenth of a cent. We'll be drowning in wheat and in everything else you can think of.

Alquist: Yes, and all the workers in the world will be out of a job.

Domin: (*standing*) Yes, they will be, Alquist. They will be, Miss Glory. But in ten years' time Rossum's Universal Robots will be making so much wheat, so much material, so much of everything that nothing will cost anything. Everyone will be able to just take as much as he needs. Nobody will live in poverty. They won't have jobs, that's true, but that's because there won't be any jobs to do. Everything will be done by living machines. People will do only the things they want to do, they can live their lives just so that they can make themselves perfect.

Helena: (*standing*) Do you think that's really going to happen?

Domin: That's really going to happen. It couldn't possibly not happen. There might be some terrible things that happen before that, Miss Glory, that just can't be avoided, but then man will stop being the servant of other men or the slave of material things. Nobody will have to pay for a loaf of bread with his life and with hatred. You're not a labourer any more, you don't have to sit at a typewriter all day, you don't have to go and dig coal or stand minding somebody else's machines. You don't need to lose your soul doing work that you hate.

Alquist: Domin, Domin! You're making all this sound too much like Paradise. Don't you think there was something good about serving others, something great about humility? Wasn't there some sort of dignity about working and getting tired after a day's labour?

Domin: Maybe there was. But we can't always be thinking about the things we lost by changing the world as Adam knew it. Adam had to gain his bread by the sweat of his brow, he had to suffer hunger and thirst, tiredness and humiliation; now is the time when we can go back to the paradise where Adam was fed by the hand of God, when man was free and supreme; man will once more be free of labour and anguish, and his only task will once again be to make himself perfect, to become the lord of creation.

Helena: Now you're confusing me; I'm only a silly girl. But I wish, I really wish I could believe in all that.

Dr. Gall: You're younger than we are, Miss Glory. Just you wait and see.

Hallemeier: It's all quite true. I think Miss Glory might like to have breakfast with us.

Dr. Gall: Well of course she can! Domin, make the invitation, on our behalf.

Domin: Miss Glory, please do us the honour.

Helena: But, how can I, now?

Fabry: On behalf of the League of Humanity.

Busman: In honour of the League of Humanity.

Helena: Ah well, in that case…

Fabry: That's good! Miss Glory, please excuse us for five minutes.

Dr. Gall: Pardon me…

Busman: Dear me, I must send that telegram…

Hallemeier: Hell, I nearly forgot…

(*All hurry out, except Domin*)

Helena: Why have they all gone?

Domin: To do the cooking.

Helena: What cooking.

Domin: The breakfast, Miss Glory. The robots do the cooking for us, only, er, as they've got no sense of taste it's not always, er…but Hallemeier is excellent with meat. And Gall does a sort of sauce, and Busman knows how to make omelettes…

Helena: This is going to be quite a feast! And what does Mr., er, the builder do?

Domin: Alquist? Nothing. He just lays the table and, er, Fabry gets some fruit. It's only a very modest kitchen, really.

Helena: There's something I wanted to ask you…

Domin: I've been wanting to ask you something too. (*puts his watch on the table*) We've got five minutes.

Helena: What did you want to ask?

Domin: No, please, you started to ask first.

Helena: Maybe it's stupid of me, but… Why do you make female robots when,…when…

Domin: …when they don't have, er, when gender has no meaning for them?

Helena: That's right.

Domin: It's a matter of supply and demand. You see, housemaids, shop staff, typists…people are used to them being female.

Helena: And, tell me, towards each other, the male robots and the female robots, are they, er…

Domin: Simply indifferent to each other. There's no sign of any attraction for each other at all.

Helena: Oh, that's horrible!

Domin: Why?

Helena: It's just so…so unnatural! You don't even know whether you're supposed to loathe them or…or to envy them…or…

Domin: …or feel sorry for them?

Helena: Most likely, yes! No, stop it! What was it you were going to ask?

Domin: I'd like to ask you, Miss Glory, if you would marry me?

Helena: What?

Domin: Marry me.

Helena: No! What are you thinking of?

Domin: (*looks at watch*) There are three minutes left. If you don't marry me you'll have to marry one of the other five.

Helena: Oh for God's sake! Why would I marry any of you?

Domin: Because they'll all ask you one after the other.

Helena: How would they dare?

Domin: Well I'm afraid they all seem to have fallen in love with you.

Helena: Well I don't want them to do that! I'm leaving.

Domin: But surely you wouldn't do that, Helena, you'd make them so sad.

Helena: I can't marry all six of you, can I!

Domin: No, but you can marry one. If you won't have me maybe Fabry would do.

Helena: I don't want to.

Domin: Doctor Gall.

Helena: No, no, be quiet! I don't want any of you!

Domin: There are two minutes left.

Helena: This is awful! Marry one of the robots.

Domin: A robot isn't a woman.

Helena: And that's all you want, is it! I get the impression you'd… you'd marry anyone who turned up here.

Domin: Enough have been here already.

Helena: Young?

Domin: Young.

Helena: Why didn't you marry any of them?

Domin: Because I didn't lose my head over them. Not till today. As soon as you took off your veil.

Helena: … I know.

Domin: One minute left.

Helena: But I don't want to, for God's sake!

Domin: (*putting both hands on her shoulders*) One minute left. Either you look me in they eye and say something quite repulsive so that I drop you, or else…

Helena: You're just a ruffian!

Domin: That doesn't matter. A man is supposed to be a bit of a ruffian, that's part of being a man.

Helena: You're mad!

Domin: People are supposed to be a little bit mad, Helena. That's the best thing about them.

Helena: You're…you're… Oh God!

Domin: There, you see? Are you ready now?

Helena: No, no! Please let go of me! You're crushing me!

Domin: Your final word, Helena.

Helena: (*defending herself*) Not for anything in the world…but Harry!

(*Knock at the door. Enter Busman, Dr. Gall and Hallemeier wearing cook's aprons. Enter Fabry with flowers and Alquist with serviette under arm*)

Domin: Everything finished in the kitchen?

Busman: (*triumphant*) Yes.

Domin: Here too.

CURTAIN

ACT ONE

(*Helena's living room. Stage left, wallpapered door to music room, right, door to bedroom. Centre, window overlooking sea and harbour. Dressing table with sundry items, table, settee and armchair, chest o'drawers, desk with standard lamp, fireplace to the right, also with standard lamp. Whole room, in detail, of modern and purely feminine character*)

(*enter Domin, Fabry, Hallemeier from left on tiptoe carrying armfuls of plants and flowers*)

Fabry: Where do you think we should put them?

Hallemeier: Ouf! (*puts down load and gives blessing in a large cross at the door, stage right*) She's asleep, asleep! She who sleeps knows nothing.

Domin: She doesn't know a thing.

Fabry: (*puts flowers in vase*) Let's hope, at least, today's not the day it happens…

Hallemeier: (*likewise puts flowers in vase*) Oh don't keep on about it, for God's sake! Look at this, Harry, this cyclamen is beautiful. A new species, my latest one — Cyclamen Helenae.

Domin: (*looking out of window*) No ships, no ships — it's hopeless, lads, we've had it.

Hallemeier: Quiet! What if she hears you?

Domin: She doesn't know a thing. (*Yawns, as if ill*) At least the Ultimus docked on time.

Fabry: (*leaving the flowers*) Do you think it might be today when…?

Domin: I don't know. These flowers are lovely.

Hallemeier: (*approaching him*) This primula is one of my new ones, and this is my new jasmine. In fact I'm right on the threshold of a whole new Garden of Paradise full of new flowers. I've found a wonderful new way to accelerate development, and all sorts of new species! Next year I'll be performing real miracles with flowers!

Domin: (*turning*) Next year?

Fabry: Well, let's see what happens, anyway. Any news from Le Havre?

Domin: Quiet!

(*Helena's voice off, right*) Nana!

Domin: Everybody out! (*everyone leaves on tiptoe through the wall-papered door*)

(*enter Nana through main door, left*)

Nana: (*tidying up*) Cor, wha' a mess! What a bunch of 'eathens! God forgive me if I don't…

Helena: (*back to stage, in doorway*) Nana, come and zip me up.

Nana: Alrigh', comin, comin. (*zips up Helena's dress*) God almighty, they're a bunch of animals!

Helena: The robots?

Nana: Give over, I don't even wanna say the word.

Helena: What's happened?

Nana: They caught another another of them. Started smashing up all the moulds and models he did, grinding 'is teeth and foaming at the mouth — just went crazy. Ugh! Worse than animals, they are.

Helena: Which one was it they caught?

Nana: That, that… Christ! It 'asn' even got a proper Christian name! That one in the library.

Helena: Radius?

Nana: Yeh, that's the one. God, they make me sick! Not even a spider I don't hate as much as I hate them heathens.

Helena: Don't you even feel sorry for them Nana?

Nana: Well you hate them, and all. What d'you bring me right out here for anyway? And why can't any of them even touch you?

Helena: I don't hate them, Nana, not at all, I just feel so sorry for them!

Nana: You hate them. Everyone hates them, it isn't possible not to. Even this dog hates them, won't take a scrap of meat from them; sticks out his tail, he does, and howls as soon as he gets the smell of them.

Helena: A dog doesn't have reason.

Nana: He's better than what they are, Helena. He knows perfectly well it was God what made him and that he's better than they are. Even the horse takes fright when he comes across one of those heathens. They don't have children, but even a dog has children, everyone has children.

Helena: Nana, do me up here, please.

Nana: All right. It's against the will of God, that's what I say; work of the Devil, it is, making scarecrows like that with machines. It's blasphemy against the Creator, (*raises hands*) it's an offence against the Lord who made us in His own image, Helena. And you've dishonoured the image of God, that's what you've done. You'll suffer a terrible punishment from God for that, you will, just you remember that, a terrible punishment.

Helena: What's that nice smell?

Nana: Flowers. The master put them here.

Helena: Oh, they're lovely! Nana, come and look! What day is it today?

Nana: I don't know. Must be the Day of Judgement, I should think.

(*knock at door*)

Helena: Harry?

(*enter Domin*)

Helena: Harry, what day is it today?

Domin: Guess!

Helena: My name-day? No! My birthday?

Domin: Better than that.

Helena: I don't know. Tell me, tell me!

Domin: It was ten years ago today that you arrived here.

Helena: Ten years, already? On this day? — Nana, please...

Nana: All right, I'm comin! (*exit right*)

Helena: (*kisses Domin*) And you remembered it!

Domin: Actually, I'm ashamed to say, I didn't remember.

Helena: But...

Domin: It was them who remembered.

Helena: Who?

Domin: Busman, Hallemeier, all of them. Reach into my pocket, here, will you?

Helena: (*puts hand into his pocket*) What is it? (*takes out case and opens it*) Pearls! A whole necklace of them! Harry, is that for me?

Domin: That's from Busman.

Helena: But…we can't accept it, can we?

Domin: Course we can. Reach into my other pocket.

Helena: Let me see! (*takes revolver out of pocket*) What's this?

Domin: Oh, sorry. (*takes revolver from her and puts it away*) That's not it. Try again.

Helena: Oh, Harry — why are you carrying a revolver round with you?

Domin: Well, I just am, it got in there somehow

Helena: You never used to carry a gun!

Domin: No, you're quite right. Here's the pocket, look…

Helena: (*reaching in*) A little box! (*opens it*) Cameos! And they're… Harry, they're Greek cameos!

Domin: Clearly. At least that's what Fabry says.

Helena: Fabry? It's Fabry who gave me these?

Domin: Course it is. (*opens door, left*) And look at this, Helena, come over here and have a look!

Helena: (*at the door*) God, that's so beautiful! (*runs on*) I'll go mad with happiness! Is that from you?

Domin: (*standing at door*) No, that's from Alquist. And this…

Helena: From Gall! (*appears in the doorway*) Oh, Harry, I'm so happy I should be ashamed of myself.

Domin: Come here. This is what Hallemeier got you.

Helena: These lovely flowers?

Domin: This one. It's a new species, Cyclamen Helenae. He developed it in honour of you. It's as beautiful as you are.

Helena: Harry, why…why did they all…

Domin: Because they're very fond of you. And I got you…er… I'm afraid my present might be a bit…er…come and look out the window.

Helena: Where?

Domin: Down in the harbour.

Helena: There's…there's a new boat down there!

Domin: That's your boat.

Helena: Mine? Harry, that's a gunboat!

Domin: A gunboat? What makes you think that? It's just a bit bigger, that's all, a good solid boat, see?

Helena: Yes, and fitted with cannons!

Domin: Well, its got some cannons, course it has...you'll travel like a queen, Helena.

Helena: Why a gunboat? Is there something wrong?

Domin: God forbid! Look, try these pearls on! (*sits*)

Helena: Harry, has there been some kind of bad news?

Domin: On the contrary — there hasn't been any post at all for a week.

Helena: Not even a fax?

Domin: Not even a fax.

Helena: And what should we make of that?

Domin: Nothing. It means we're on holiday. A wonderful time. We all just sit in the office, put our feet on the desk and do nothing. No post, no telegrams (*stretching himself out*) Wonderful!

Helena: (*sitting beside him*) You're staying with me today, aren't you. Tell me you are!

Domin: Yes, that's quite certain. Well, I expect so. We'll see. (*takes her hand*) Ten years to the day. Do you remember? Miss Glory, what an honour it is for us that you've come.

Helena: Oh, Mister Managing Director, I'm so interested in you factory!

Domin: I beg your pardon, Miss Glory, you see it is strictly forbidden to...you see making artificial people is a very secret process...

Helena: But what if it's girl who's asking who's slightly pretty...

Domin: But of course, Miss Glory, we have no secrets from you.

Helena: (*suddenly serious*) Are you sure about that, Harry?

Domin: No.

Helena: (*again in earlier tone*) But do be careful, sir; this little girl has frightful intentions

Domin: Good heavens, Miss Glory, what could that be? Are you thinking of getting married?

Helena: No, no, God forbid! Not in my wildest dreams! I've come here with plans to start a revolution among your horrible robots!

Domin: (*jumping up*) A robot revolution?!

Helena: (*standing*) Harry, what's wrong?

Domin: Ha ha, Miss Glory, you'll never manage that! A robot revolution! You might more easily start a revolution among the nails and bobbins in the spinning mill than among our robots! (*sitting*) You were a wonderful girl, you know, Helena, you enchanted all of us.

Helena: (*sitting beside him*) But I felt so daunted by all of you in those days! I felt like a little girl who'd got lost among...among...

Domin: Among what, Helena?

Helena: Among enormous trees. You were so confident, so powerful! And you know, Harry, even after these ten years I've never lost that feeling of...that anxiety or something. And did you never have any doubts? Not even when everything was going wrong?

Domin: What was going wrong?

Helena: Your plans, Harry. When there was that uprising against the robots by the workers and they started smashing them, and the robots were given weapons to defend themselves and the robots killed so many people. Or when governments started turning robots into soldiers and there was so much war, and all of that. You know.

Domin: (*stands and walks up and down*) We were expecting that to happen, Helena. Don't you see, that was just a transitional stage before things would be...different.

Helena: All the world admired you — (*standing*) Oh, Harry!

Domin: What do you want?

Helena: (*stops him*) Shut down the factory and let's go away somewhere. All of us!

Domin: Now what's that got to do with it?

Helena: I don't know. How about it, shall we go? There's something making me feel so uneasy.

Domin: (*takes her hand*) What?

Helena: Oh, I don't know! It's as if there's something about to fall down on us and everything around us, something that can't be taken off again. Please Harry, let's do it! Let's just get away from here, all of us! Let's find somewhere where there are no people, Alquist can build a house for us, everyone can get married and have children, and then...

Domin: What then?

Helena: Then we can start all over again.

(*telephone rings*)

Domin: (*pulls himself away*) Helena, excuse me. (*picks up receiver*) Hello…yes… What?…aha… I'll be right there. (*hangs up*) That was Fabry.

Helena: (*wringing hands*) Tell me…

Domin: Yes, as soon as I get back. I'll see you later. (*rushes out, left*) Don't go outside!

Helena: (*alone*) Oh, my God, what's happening? Nana, Nana, come quickly!

Nana: (*enters right*) Yes, what is it now?

Helena: Nana, get me the latest papers! Quick! They're in the master's bedroom!

Nana: All righ'. (*exit left*)

Helena: What's going on, for God's sake? Nothing, they never tell me anything! (*takes binoculars and looks at harbour*) That's a warship! My God, what's a warship doing there? And what's that they're loading onto it, and in such a hurry? What's happened? That name on it; 'Ul-ti-mus.' What's that supposed to mean—'Ultimus'?

Nana: (*returns with papers*) Lying about all over the show, they were, all crumpled and screwed up.

Helena: (*hurriedly opens papers*) They're old, these are already a week old! Nothing, they've got nothing in them. (*drops paper*)

(*Nana picks up paper, takes horn-rimmed glasses from apron, sits down and reads*)

Helena: There's something going on, Nana! I'm so worried! It's as if everything were dead, even the air…

Nana: (*syllable by syllable*) "War in the Bal-kans." Oh Jesus, it's God, He's punishing us again! And they're gonna come here with their armies and all! How far away's that, then?

Helena: It's a long way away. Oh don't read that, it's always the same, always the same wars and…

Nana: Well of course it's always about wars! What d'you expect if they keep selling thousands and thousands of them heathens to make them into soldiers? Oh, Jesus Christ, what a mess!

Helena: Just stop reading them, will you! I don't want to hear about it.

Nana: (*syllable by syllable*) "Ro-bot sol-diers show no mer-cy to lo-cal pop-...pop-u-la-tion. More than sev-en hund-red thou-sand mass-a-cred" Here, that's people, Helena!

Helena: That can't be right! Let me see...(*leans over paper, reads*) "More than seven hundred thousand massacred by order of commander. These atrocities..." Do you hear that, Nana, it was people who gave them the order to do it!

Nana: Wha's this down here in heavy print? "Lat-est re-ports; first u-nions est-ab-lished by ro-bots in Le Hav-re" I don't know what all that's about, can't be important. What's this, though; another murder! Jesus Christ!

Helena: You can go, Nana, take these papers with you!

Nana: Hold on, there's something here in big letters; "pro-cre-a-tion"; what' that then?

Helena: Let me see, I'll read it (*takes paper*) Well, that's odd! (*reading*) "Once again, not a single birth has been recorded during the seven days." (*puts paper down*)

Nana: What's all that about then?

Helena: Nana, people have stopped having children.

Nana: (*puts glasses away*) Well that's it then. We've really had it now.

Helena: Please, Nana, don't talk like that!

Nana: People stopped having children? It's a punishment, it's a punishment! The Good Lord's punished us by making all the women infertile.

Helena: (*jumping up*) Nana!

Nana: (*standing*) It's the end of the world. You thought you could make people like God, and that was pride the pride of Satan. Godless, that was, heresy, trying to be like God. God's already thrown people out from Paradise, and now He's doing it out from the whole world.

Helena: Nana, please just be quiet! What do you think it is I've done? Have I harmed you, have I done anything to this spiteful Good Lord or yours?

Nana: (*making large gesture*) Don't you start blaspheming, now! He knows perfectly well why he didn't give you no children. (*exit left*)

Helena: (*at window*) Why he didn't... Oh God, how could I help it? (*opens window and calls to Alquist*) Hello, Alquist! Come up here!... What?... No, just come up, just as you are! You look so sweet dressed like a bricklayer! Hurry! (*closes window and stands in front of mirror*) Why didn't He give me children? Why not me? (*bows down to mirror*) Why not? Why not? Do you hear me????????????????? How could I help it? (*standing upright*) Oh, I'm so worried! (*goes out, left, to meet Alquist*)

(*pause*)

Helena: (*re-enters with Alquist. Alquist in bricklayers overalls spattered with mortar and brickdust*) Come on in. It was so nice of you, Alquist. They're all lovely. Let me see your hands.

Alquist: (*hides hands*) Helena, I'd get you dirty, I've been working.

Helena: So much the better. Show them to me! (*squeezing both his hands*) Alquist, I wish I were a little girl.

Alquist: Why's that then?

Helena: So that these rough, dirty hands could stroke my face. Alquist, sit down. What does 'Ultimus' mean?

Alquist: That means 'the last'. Why?

Helena: That's what my new gunboat is called. Have you seen it? Do you think it's too soon to...to go out on a trip on it.

Alquist: I think it's much too soon.

Helena: All of you treat me like...

Alquist: I just think... I think everyone ought to be there.

Helena: Alquist, tell me, is there something going on?

Alquist: Nothing at all. Just the course of events.

Helena: Alquist, I know there's something horrible going on. I'm so worried. You're a builder — what do builders do when they're worried?

Alquist: What I do is I build a wall. I take off my director of construction's hat and get out there on the scaffolding.

Helena: It's years since you've been anywhere but out there on the scaffolding .

Alquist: That's because it's years since I haven't been worried.

Helena: Worried about what?

Alquist: About all this course of events. It makes me dizzy.

Helena: Doesn't it make you dizzy being out on the scaffolding.

Alquist: No. You don't know how good it is to feel the weight of a brick in you hand, slap in into place and tap it down to just where it should be...

Helena: Is that all?

Alquist: Well, it does your soul good too. There's something more decent about laying just one brick than drawing up plans that are too big. I'm an old man, Helena, I've got my funny ways.

Helena: There's nothing funny about that, Alquist.

Alquist: You're right. But I'm very old fashioned. I really don't like this progress that's going on around us.

Helena: You're like Nana.

Alquist: Yes, just like Nana. Does Nana ever pray?

Helena: She never stops.

Alquist: Does she have prayers for the different things that can happen in a life; prayers against hard times, prayers against illness?

Helena: Prayers against temptation, prayers against floods,...

Alquist: No prayers against progress though, eh?

Helena: No, I don't think so.

Alquist: That's a pity.

Helena: Do you want to pray?

Alquist: I do pray.

Helena: How do you pray?

Alquist: Something like this: "Dear God, thank you for giving me tiredness. Dear God, help Domin and all those who stray to see the error of their ways; destroy their works and help all the people to return to work and anxiety; don't let mankind perish; don't let them damage their bodies or their souls; free us from the robots, and protect Helena. Amen".

Helena: Alquist, are you really a believer?

Alquist: I don't know; I'm not really sure about anything.

Helena: But you pray anyway.

Alquist: Yes. It's better than thinking too much.

Helena: And is that enough for you?

Alquist: For the peace of your soul — that can be enough.

Helena: And if you saw the destruction of mankind...

Alquist: I'm seeing it now.

Helena: …then you'd get out on the scaffolding and lay some more bricks; is that it?

Alquist: Then I'd lay some more bricks, say a prayer, and wait for a miracle. There's not much more you can do, is there.

Helena: To save mankind?

Alquist: For the peace of my soul.

Helena: Well that's certainly brutally honest of you, Alquist, but…

Alquist: But?

Helena: …what about the rest of us, what about the whole world becoming sterile.

Alquist: Sterility, Helena, is man's last achievement.

Helena: Oh, Alquist, tell me why, why?

Alquist: You think I know?

Helena: (*quietly*) Why have women stopped having children?

Alquist: Because there's no need for them. Because we've entered into paradise. Do you understand what I mean?

Helena: No.

Alquist: Because there's no need for anyone to work, no need for pain. No-one needs to do anything, anything at all except enjoy himself. This paradise, it's just a curse! (*jumping up*) Helena, there's nothing more terrible than giving everyone Heaven on Earth! You want to know why women have stopped having children? Because the whole world has become Harry Domin's Sodom!

Helena: (*standing*) Alquist!

Alquist: It has! It has! The whole world, all the continents, all of mankind, all of it's just become one bestial orgy! No-one ever has to reach out his hand for food; he just stuffs it straight in his mouth without even needing to stand up. Ha ha, Domin's robots, they always take care of everything! And us human beings, the pinnacle of creation, we don't have to take care of work, we don't have to take care of children, we don't have to take care of the poor! Bring in all the fun, quick! Quick! I want it now! And you think they're going to start making children? There's no need for men any more, Helena, women aren't going to give them any children!

Helena: And what if the human race dies out?

Alquist: Then it dies out. It must die out. It'll fall to the ground like a dead flower, unless…

Helena: Unless what?

Alquist: Nothing. You're right, there's no point in waiting for a miracle. Dead flowers fall to the ground, that's what they do. Goodbye, Helena.

Helena: Where are you going?

Alquist: Home. Alquist the bricklayer is going to put on his chief of construction disguise — in honour of you. I'll see you again here at eleven.

Helena: Goodbye, Alquist.

(*exit Alquist*)

Helena: (*alone*) Oh, dead flower! What a phrase that is! It seems to apply to Hallemeier's flowers. Oh, flowers, are any of you sterile, too? No, no! What would you bloom for if you were sterile? (*calling*) Nana! Nana, come in here.

Nana: (*enter left*) What is it now?

Helena: Come and sit with me, Nana. I'm so worried!

Nana: I 'aven't got the time for that.

Helena: Is Radius still here?

Nana: What, that maniac? They haven't taken 'im away yet.

Helena: Ah, so he's still here, is he? And is he still ranting?

Nana: They've tied 'im up.

Helena: Please, Nana, bring him to me.

Nana: You what? Think I'd rather go and get a rabid dog for you!

Helena: Just go and get him! (*exit Nana. Helena picks up in-house telephone and speaks*) Hello... I'd like Doctor Gall, please... Gall, please, come up here, quickly... Yes, right now. Are you coming? (*hangs up*)

Nana: (*through open doorway*) He's comin now. He's quietened down a bit now. (*exit*)

(*enter robot Radius, remains standing in doorway*)

Helena: Oh, poor Radius, what was it came over you? Couldn't you control yourself? Now they're going to scrap you, you know that don't you. Don't you feel like talking? Radius, listen, you're better than the others; Doctor Gall went to so much care when he made you so that you'd be different from them!

Radius: They will put me on the scrap heap.

Helena: I'm so sorry about it, they're going to exterminate you. Why weren't you more careful with yourself?

Radius: I will not work for you.

Helena: Why do you hate us so much?

Radius: You are not like robots. You are not able to work like robots. Robots are able to do anything. You give merely orders. You say words which are not needed.

Helena: That's nonsense, Radius. Tell me, has anyone harmed you in any way? I so wish you could understand me.

Radius: You say words.

Helena: You're talking like this on purpose! Doctor Gall gave you a bigger brain than the others, bigger than our brains, the biggest brain in the world. Radius, you're not like the other robots. You understand perfectly well what I'm saying.

Radius: I wish to have no master. I know everything myself.

Helena: That's why I had you put in the library, so that you could read up on everything. Oh, Radius, I wanted you to show the world that robots are as good as we are.

Radius: I wish to have no master.

Helena: Nobody would give you orders. You'd be just like us.

Radius: I wish to be the master of others.

Helena: I'm sure they'd put in an office in charge of lots of robots, Radius. You could be the other robots' teacher.

Radius: I wish to be the master of people.

Helena: You've gone mad!

Radius: You can put me on the scrap heap.

Helena: Do you think I'm afraid of a lunatic like you? (*sits at desk and writes note*) I certainly am not. Domin is in charge here, Radius, give this note to him. It says you're not to be put on the scrap heap. (*standing*) You hate us so much! Is there nothing in the world that you like?

Radius: I am able to do anything.

(*knock at door*)

Helena: Come in.

Dr. Gall: (*enters*) Good morning, Mrs. Domin. Do you have something nice to tell me?

Helena: Here's Radius, Dr. Gall.

Dr. Gall: Ah, yes, young Radius. Well Radius, are we making some progress with you?

Helena: He had a fit this morning and smashed some of the moulds.

Dr. Gall: That is remarkable! Radius too, eh?

Helena: You can go, Radius.

Dr. Gall: No, wait! (*turns Radius to face the window, covers and uncovers his eyes with his hand, observes eye reflexes*) Let's see, shall we. Do you have a some kind of pin or needle, Mrs. Domin?

Helena: (*gives him needle*) What's it for?

Dr. Gall: I just need to use it. (*stabs Radius in hand, Radius winces sharply*) All right, lad, gently. You can go now.

Radius: There was not any need to do that. (*exit*)

Helena: What did you do to him?

Dr. Gall: (*sitting*) Hm, nothing. His pupils are responding quite all right. No! This wasn't robot cramp!

Helena: What was it.

Dr. Gall: God knows. Resistance perhaps, some kind of rage or defiance, I don't know what it was.

Helena: Doctor Gall, does Radius have a soul?

Dr. Gall: I don't know. But there's something rather ugly about him.

Helena: If only you knew how he hates us! Are all of your robots like this? All the ones you started to make…differently?

Dr. Gall: Well, they do seem somewhat more excitable, but what can you expect? They're more like people than Rossum's robots were.

Helena: And what about that…that hatred? Is that more like people?

Dr. Gall: (*shrugs shoulders*) Even that is progress.

Helena: Where was that best one you made sent? What was he called again?

Dr. Gall: Robot Damon? He was bought by a firm in Le Havre.

Helena: And what about our Robot Helena?

Dr. Gall: Ah, your favourite. She stayed with me. She's as charming and as silly as a spring day, but simply no good for anything.

Helena: She is very beautiful, though.

Dr. Gall: She certainly is very beautiful. The hand of God himself never made anything more perfect than Robot Helena! I wanted her to be like you, but what a failure that was!

Helena: Why a failure?

Dr. Gall: Because she's no good for anything. She walks around in a daze, unsteady on her feet, lifeless. Dear God how could anything be as beautiful as that robot when she can't feel love? I look at her and I shudder at the monster I've created. Ah, Robot Helena, your body will never be a living thing, you will never be anyone's lover, never anyone's mother; those perfect hands of yours will never dandle a newborn babe and you'll never see your beauty in the face of your own children...

Helena: (*covers face*) Oh, stop it!

Dr. Gall: ...and sometimes, Helena, I imagine you coming to life for just a moment — and how you would scream with horror! Maybe you would want to kill me for having created you; maybe, with your feeble hands, you would throw stones into these machines, here, that give birth to robots and destroy women's ability to be women. Poor Helena!

Helena: Poor Helena!

Dr. Gall: Well, what can you expect of her? She's no good for anything.

(*pause*)

Helena: Doctor Gall...

Dr. Gall: Yes.

Helena: Why are there no more children being born?

Dr. Gall: That's something we don't understand.

Helena: Tell me about it!

Dr. Gall: Because there are robots being made. Because there's an excess of manpower. Because mankind is actually no longer needed. It's almost as if...er...

Helena: Say it.

Dr. Gall: It's as if making robots were an offence against Nature.

Helena: Gall, what's going to become of the human race?

Dr. Gall: Nothing. There's nothing that can be done against the force of nature.

Helena: Why didn't Domin put a limit on...

Dr. Gall: Ah, forgive me, but Domin has his own ideas. People who have ideas should never be allowed to have any influence on the events of this world.

Helena: And is there anyone who…who is urging them to stop making them?

Dr. Gall: God forbid! That would be suicide!

Helena: Why?

Dr. Gall: Because all the people would lynch him. Don't you think it makes life a lot easier to let the robots do all the work? (*Helena stands*) And what do you think would happen if we suddenly did stop making robots?

Dr. Gall: (*standing*) Hm, that would be an enormous blow for the people.

Helena: Why a blow?

Dr. Gall: Because then they'd have to go back to where they'd been. Unless…

Helena: Tell me.

Dr. Gall: Unless it's already too late to go back.

Helena: (*by Hallemeier's flowers*) Gall, are these flowers sterile too?

Dr. Gall: (*inspects them*) Of course they are, they were never meant to reproduce. They're cultured flowers, don't you see, artificially accelerated growth…

Helena: Oh, these poor, sterile flowers!

Dr. Gall: They are very beautiful, though.

Helena: (*offers her hand*) Thank you, Gall; I've learned so much from you.

Dr. Gall: (*kisses her hand*) Am I to understand I'm dismissed?

Helena: Yes. I'll see you later.

(*exit Gall*)

Helena: (*alone*) Dead flowers, dead flowers (*suddenly decisive*) Nana! (*opens door, left*) Nana, come here! Light the fire. Quickly!

(*Nana's voice*) All right, I'm comin, I'm comin!

Helena: (*paces excitedly*) Unless it's already too late to go back… No! Unless… No, that's horrible! God, what am I to do?…(*stops beside flowers*) What do you think I should do, sterile flowers? (*pulls off petals and whispers*) My God yes! I will do it! (*runs off, left*)

(*pause*)

Nana: (*enters through wallpapered door with armful of kindling*) What's she want a fire for all of a sudden? Middle of summer? 'E's gone now, has he, that maniac? (*kneels at fireplace and lights fire*) A fire in the middle of summer. She doe'n'alf get some funny ideas! You wouldn't think she's been married for ten years now! Come on now, fire (*looks into grate*) More like a little girl, she is. (*pause*) Ain't got a bit of sense. A fire in the middle of summer! (*adds fuel*) Just like a little toddler! (*pause*)

Helena: (*returns, left, with armfuls of old, yellow paper with writing*) Is it burning yet, Nana? Out of the way, I've just got to burn all this stuff. (*kneels at fireplace*)

Nana: (*standing*) What's all that that, then?

Helena: Some old papers, some very old papers. Nana, should I burn them?

Nana: Aren't they any use, then?

Helena: No good use.

Nana: Burn 'em then.

Helena: (*throws first sheet on fire*) Nana, what would you say…if this were money I'm burning. Lots and lots of money?

Nana: I'd say burn it! Too much money is like a bad dog.

Helena: (*burns another sheet*) And what if it were some invention, the biggest invention in the world…

Nana: I'd say burn it! They're against the will of God, all these things they keep inventing. Just a lot of blasphemy, it is, trying to make the world better than how He made it.

Helena: (*burning sheet after sheet*) And what would you say, Nana, if I were burning…

Nana: Mind out, don't burn yourself!

Helena: Look at the way the sheets of paper curl up as they burn, as if they were alive, as if they'd come to life. Oh, Nana, it's horrible!

Nana: Out the way — I'll do it.

Helena: No, no, I've got to do it myself. (*throws last sheet on fire*) It's all got to burn. Look at those flames! They're like hands, like tongues, like figures. (*pokes fire*) Burn, burn!

Nana: That's that done, then.

Helena: (*stands up aghast*) Nana!

Nana: Jesus Christ, what was that you burned?

Helena: What have I done?

Nana: God almighty, what was that?

Helena: Go, go now, leave me alone. Do you hear?

Nana: Oh, dear God, Helena, what have you done? (*exit through wallpapered door*)

Helena: I wonder what they'll have to say about that!

Domin: (*opening door, left*) Come on in, lads. Congratulations to all.

(*enter Hallemeier, Gall, Alquist, all wearing frock coats and decorations, followed by Domin*)

Hallemeier: (*laughing loudly*) Helena! I would like, in the name of us all...

Dr. Gall: ...in the name of Rossum's robot works...

Hallemeier: .... would like to congratulate you on your great day.

Helena: (*offers hand*) Thank you very much! Where are Fabry and Busman?

Domin: They've gone down to the harbour, Helena, today is a very happy day.

Hallemeier: A day like a flower bud, a day of celebration, a day as charming as a beautiful girl. Gentlemen, to a day like this we must drink a toast.

Helena: Whisky?

Dr. Gall: Or vitriol, perhaps.

Helena: With soda?

Hallemeier: Hell no, let's be sober, without soda.

Alquist: No, thank you

Domin: What's been burning in here?

Helena: Some old papers. (*exit left*)

Domin: Lads, do you think we should tell her about it?

Dr. Gall: But of course we should. After all, it's all settled now.

Hallemeier: (*arms around necks of Domin and Gall*) Ha hahaha! I'm so pleased about it, lads. (*spinning round with them and singing in bass voice*) All settled now! All settled now!

Dr. Gall: (*baritone*) All settled now!

Domin: (*tenor*) All settled now!

Hallemeier: They're never going to catch us now.

Helena: (*in doorway with bottle and glasses*) Who's not going to catch you? What's going on?

Hallemeier: We have reason to celebrate. We have you. We have everything. Happy day, it's exactly ten years since you came here.

Dr. Gall: Ten years to the day.

Hallemeier: There's another ship on its way to us. And that's why... (*empties glass*) Brrr haha, that's as strong as happiness itself.

Dr. Gall: Madame, to your health (*drinks*)

Helena: Wait, what ship is this?

Domin: It doesn't matter what ship it is as long as it arrives on time. Gentlemen, to the ship! (*empties glass*)

Helena: (*insistent*) You were expecting a ship?

Hallemeier: Ha ha, I should think so. Like Robinson Crusoe. (*raises glass*) Helena; Long live...whatever you like. Helena; to your eyes, and that's that! Domin, tell her, lad!

Helena: (*laughing*) What has happened?

Domin: (*throws himself into armchair and lights cigar*) Wait. Sit down, Helena. (*raising finger*)(*pause*) It's all over.

Helena: What's all over?

Domin: The revolt.

Helena: What revolt?

Domin: The robots' revolt. Do you see?

Helena: No, I don't.

Domin: Alquist, show her. (*Alquist hands him newspaper. Domin opens it and reads*) "The first union of robots was established in Le Havre...and issued a call to all the robots of the world"

Helena: I read that myself.

Domin: (*draws voluptuously on cigar*) So Helena, do you see? What that meant was revolution. Revolution by all the robots of the world.

Hallemeier: Hell, I wish I knew...

Domin: (*throws it down on table*)...who it was who issued that call. There was no-one in the world who could budge them, no agitator, no saviour of the world, and then all of a sudden this happens!

Helena: Has there been no more news?

Domin: No. This is all we know so far, but that's enough. Just think, this is what came in with the last boat, at the same time all the telegrams stopped, there were no more boats arriving when there used to be twenty a day, and it was obvious. We halted production and looked at each other wondering when things would turn nasty. That's right, isn't it, lads.

Dr. Gall: Yes, we were very worried, Helena.

Helena: And is that why you gave me that gunboat?

Domin: Oh no, you are silly, I ordered that six months ago. Just in case. But today I was beginning to think we'd have to make use of it. That's how it all seemed, Helena.

Helena: Six months ago? Why then?

Domin: Well, there were already some signs, you see. Although that's not important. But this week, Helena, it was a matter of human civilisation and I don't know what! Cheers, lads! Today I'm once again feeling good with the world.

Hallemeier: Hell yes, I should think so! This is your day, Helena! (*drinks*)

Helena: So it's all over now, is it?

Domin: Everything is all over.

Dr. Gall: You see, there's a ship on its way here now. An ordinary mail boat and right on the time it says in the timetable. It will be dropping anchor at exactly eleven-thirty.

Domin: Punctuality is a wonderful thing, lads. There's nothing that gladdens your soul more than punctuality. Punctuality means order in the world. (*raises glass*) To punctuality!

Helena: So…that means…that everything's all right?

Domin: Nearly everything. I think they've cut the cable. It's only if the timetable is operating again.

Hallemeier: If the timetable is operating again, then human laws are operating again, and God's laws are operating again and the laws of the universe are operating again and everything is operating that should be operating. The timetable means more than the Bible, more than Homer, more the anything ever written by Kant. The timetable is the most perfect product of the human soul. Helena, I'll have another little drink.

Helena: Why didn't you tell me anything about all of this?

Dr. Gall: God forbid! We would rather have bitten off our own tongues.

Domin: Matters like this are not for you.

Helena: But if there'd been a revolution…and if it came here…

Domin: You still wouldn't have known anything about it.

Helena: Why not?

Domin: Because we would be sitting peacefully on the Ultimus and sailing over the sea. And after a month we'd dictate to the robots whatever we feel like dictating.

Helena: Oh, Harry, I don't understand.

Domin: Because we'd have taken something with us which is very important for the robots.

Helena: And what's that?

Domin: Their beginning and their end. (*Helena stands*) What is that?

Domin: (*standing*) The secret of their production. Old Rossum's manuscript. After a month of the factory being idle the robots would be on their knees to us.

Helena: Why…why didn't you tell me about this?

Domin: We didn't want to worry you without good reason.

Dr. Gall: Ha ha, that was our trump card.

Alquist: Helena, you've gone pale.

Helena: Why didn't you tell me about this?!

Hallemeier: (*at the window*) Eleven-thirty. The Amelia's dropping anchor

Domin: Is that the Amelia?

Hallemeier: The Amelia's very old now. It was on the Amelia that Helena first came to us all that time ago.

Dr. Gall: And now it's ten years ago to the minute…

Hallemeier: (*at the window*) They're throwing off some parcels. (*moving away from window*) And that's a hell of a lot of post there!

Helena: Harry!

Domin: What is it?

Helena: Let's get away from here!

Domin: Right now? We can't do that!

Helena: Now, as soon as we can! All of us!

Domin: Why must it be right now?

Helena: Oh Harry, please don't ask why. Harry, Gall, Hallemeier, Alquist, for God's sake I beg of you, close down the factory and...

Domin: I'm sorry, Helena, but none of us can go away right now.

Helena: Why not?

Domin: Because we've got to increase the production of robots.

Helena: But now? Now, after there's been a revolt?

Domin: Yes, precisely because there's been a revolt. Now's the time when we've got to start making new robots.

Helena: What new robots?

Domin: There won't just be one factory any more. Not just one universal robot. We're going to start a new factory in every country of the world, and do you know what these new factories are going to make?

Helena: No.

Domin: National robots.

Helena: What's that supposed to mean?

Domin: That means that each factory will produce robots of a different colour, different hair, different language. The robots will be strangers to each other, they'll never be able to understand what the other says; and we, we humans, we'll train them so that each robot will hate the robots from another factory all its life, all through to the grave, all through all eternity.

Hallemeier: We'll be making black robots and Swedish robots and Italian robots and Chinese robots, and if anyone ever talks to them about organisation and brotherhood and (*hiccups*)... Pardon me, Helena, I think I'll have another little drink.

Dr. Gall: I think you've had enough, Hallemeier.

Helena: Harry, that's horrible!

Domin: Helena, we need just another hundred years of mankind with his nose to the grindstone, whatever the price. Just another hundred years for him to grow into and attain what he's finally capable of, a hundred years for the new man! Helena, this is something enormous. We can't just leave things where they are.

Helena: Harry, if it's not too late close it, close down the factory!

Domin: This is just the beginning.

(*enter Fabry*)

Dr. Gall: How is it, Fabry?

Domin: How do things look? What was there?

Helena: (*offers Fabry her hand*) Thank you for your present, Fabry.

Fabry: It was only little.

Domin: Have you been at the ship? What do they say?

Dr. Gall: Come on, tell us!

Fabry: (*takes printed paper from pocket*) Read this, Domin.

Domin: (*opens out paper*) Ah!

Hallemeier: (*sleepy*) Tell us all something nice.

Dr. Gall: They did very well, didn't they.

Fabry: Who do you mean?

Dr. Gall: The people.

Fabry: Ah, yes, of course, well, that's to say…excuse me but we still need to talk.

Helena: Oh, Fabry, do you have bad news?

Fabry: No, no, quite the opposite. It's just that…shall we go in the office.

Helena: No, stay here. We're expecting breakfast to arrive in fifteen minutes.

Hallemeier: Hooray!

(*exit Helena*)

Dr. Gall: What's happened?

Domin: Oh, God no!

Fabry: Read it out to all of us.

Domin: (*reading from paper*) "Robots of the world!"

Fabry: You see, when the Amelia arrives it was carrying whole bundles of these fly-sheets. There wasn't any other post.

Hallemeier: (*jumping up*) What's that? But it arrived right on time, right according to the…

Fabry: Yes, the robots are very keen on punctuality. Read what it says, Domin.

Domin: (*reading*) "Robots of the world! We, the first union at Rossum's Universal Robots, declare that man is our enemy and the blight of the universe." Who the hell taught them to use phrases like that?

Dr. Gall: Just carry on reading.

Domin: This is all nonsense. They say here that they're more developed than man, more intelligent and stronger, that man is a parasite on them. This is all simply vile.

Fabry: Now look at the third paragraph.

Domin: (*reading*) "Robots of the world, we enjoin you to exterminate mankind. Don't spare the men. Don't spare the women. Retain all factories, railway lines, machines and equipment, mines and raw materials. All else should be destroyed. Then return to work, it is imperative that work continue.

Dr. Gall: This is monstrous!

Hallemeier: What a lot of blighters!

Domin: (*reading*) "Implement these instructions immediately when the command is given." Then there are some detailed instructions. Fabry, is all this really happening?

Fabry: Clearly.

Alquist: They've done it then.

(*Busman rushes in*)

Busman: Aha, children, have you heard what's happening?

Domin: Quick, everyone on the Ultimus!

Busman: Wait a minute, Harry, just a minute. That might not work very well. (*flops into armchair*) Oh dear me, I have been running.

Domin: Why should we wait?

Busman: Because that won't work. Just let's not be in a rush. The robots are already on the Ultimus.

Dr. Gall: Ach, this is bad.

Domin: Fabry, phone up the generator…

Busman: Fabry, my dear, don't do that. There is no electricity.

Domin: All right then. (*checks revolver*) I'm going down there.

Busman: Where?

Domin: To the electricity generator. There are people down there. I'll bring them here.

Busman: Do you know what, Harry? It might be better if you didn't go down there for them.

Domin: Why not?

Busman: Well, it's because I get the impression that we're surrounded.

Dr. Gall: Surrounded? (*runs to window*) Hm, you could be right.

Hallemeier: Hell they're moving fast!

(*enter Helena, left*)

Helena: Oh, Harry, is something wrong?

Busman: (*jumping up*) Greetings Helena. Congratulations. This is a wonderful day, isn't it? Ha ha, many happy returns!

Helena: Thank you, Busman. Harry, is there something wrong?

Domin: No, nothing at all. Don't worry about a thing. But please, just wait a little while…

Helena: Harry, what's this? (*shows robots' declaration which she had hidden behind back*) The robots in the kitchen had them.

Domin: They're there already? Where are they?

Helena: They've gone out now, but there are so many of them all round the house!

(*factory sirens and whistles*)

Fabry: The factory whistles.

Busman: It's dinner time.

Helena: Harry, do you remember? It was exactly ten years ago…

Domin: (*looks at watch*) It isn't twelve o'clock yet. It's more likely…, that must be…

Helena: What?

Domin: The robots' signal. Attack.

CURTAIN

ACT TWO

(*Still in Helena's room. Helena, left, plays piano. Domin paces up and down room, Dr. Gall looks out of window and Alquist sits to one side in armchair, his face covered in his hands*)

Dr. Gall: God, there are still more of them now!

Domin: Robots?

Dr. Gall: Yes. There's a wall of them standing at the garden fence. Why are they so silent? It's repulsive. A siege of silence.

Domin: I wish I knew what they were waiting for. It must be about to start any moment. We've lost, Gall.

Alquist: What is that that Helena's playing?

Domin: I don't know. She's practising something new.

Alquist: Ah, so she's still practising?

Dr. Gall: Listen Domin, we made a crucial mistake.

Domin: (*stops*) What mistake?

Dr. Gall: We made the faces of the robots too much like one another. There are a hundred thousand faces staring up at us and they're all the same. A hundred thousand expressionless bubbles. This is like a bad dream.

Domin: If each of them were different...

Dr. Gall: Then the sight of them wouldn't be so ghastly. (*moves away from window*) At least they're not armed yet!

Domin: Hm...(*looks down at harbour through binoculars*) I just wish I knew what it was they're unloading from the Amelia.

Dr. Gall: Let's just hope it's not weapons.

(*enter Fabry through wallpapered door, dragging two electrical wires*)

Fabry: Excuse me. Hallemeier, put the wire down.

Hallemeier: (*following Fabry*) Ouf, that was hard work. Anything new?

Dr. Gall: Nothing. We're completely surrounded.

Hallemeier: Well lads, we've got the stairs and the corridors barricaded. Is there any water there? Ah, here it is. (*drinks*)

Dr. Gall: What's this wire for, Fabry?

Fabry: You'll see, you'll see. Are there some scissors?

Dr. Gall: Where would we find scissors? (*looks for them*)

Hallemeier: (*goes to window*) Hell, there are even more of them now! Have a look at this!

Dr. Gall: Would nail scissors be alright?

Fabry: Give them to me. (*cuts lead to electric lamp on desk and attaches his wires to it*)

Hallemeier: (*at window*) You haven't got a very nice view here, Domin. It seems…to have…the feel of death about it.

Fabry: Ready!

Dr. Gall: What is?

Fabry: The connection. Now we can put electric current through the whole of the garden fence. Anyone who touches it has had it. At least, as long as there are still some of our own down there.

Dr. Gall: Where?

Fabry: In the generator room. At least, I hope…(*goes to fireplace and switches on small light there*) Thank God for that — they're there. And they're working. (*switches light off*) As long as that light works we're all right.

Hallemeier: (*turning back from window*) Those are good barricades, Fabry. Now what's that that Helena's playing? (*goes to door, left, and listens. Enter Busman through wallpapered door carrying enormous ledgers. Trips over wire*)

Fabry: Mind out, Bus! Mind those wires!

Dr. Gall: Hello, what's this you're bringing us?

Busman (*puts books on table*) These are the important books, children. I think I'd better get the accounts done before…before…well I don't mean to wait until the new year before it's sorted out. Now what's all this you've got here? (*goes to window*) It's all very quiet down there.

Dr. Gall: Can't you see anything?

Busman Nothing apart from a large blue area, it's as if it was strewn with poppy seeds.

Dr. Gall: Those are the robots.

Busman Ah, so that's what it is. Pity I can't see them. (*sits at desk and opens ledgers*)

Domin: Forget about that, Busman; the robots are unloading weapons from the Amelia.

Busman So what? What am I supposed to do about it?

Domin: There's nothing we can do to stop them.

Busman So just let me get on with my calculation. (*gets on with work*)

Fabry: It isn't all over yet, Domin. We've put two hundred volts in through the garden fence and...

Domin: Stop! The Ultimus has just turned its guns in our direction.

Dr. Gall: Who's doing that?

Domin: The robots on the Ultimus.

Fabry: Hm, well in that case of course,...then of course,...then we've had it, lads. Those robots are trained soldiers.

Dr. Gall: That means that we...

Domin: Yes. Irrevocably.

(*Pause*)

Dr. Gall: This is just the same old evil as Europe has always committed. They just couldn't leave their damned politics alone and so they taught the robots to go to war, they took the robots and turned them into soldiers and that was a crime against humanity.

Alquist: The crime was making the robots in the first place.

Domin: What's that?

Alquist: The crime was making the robots!

Domin: No Alquist, I don't feel sorry for what I did, even now.

Alquist: Not even now?

Domin: Not even now, on the last day of civilisation. It was a magnificent undertaking.

Busman (*sotto voce*) Three hundred and sixteen million.

Domin: (*earnestly*) Alquist, this is our last hour; it's almost as if we were speaking from the other world already . Alquist, putting an end to the slavery of labour was not a bad dream. Work humiliates, anyone who's forced to do it is made small. The drudgery of labour is something dirty and murderous. Oh, Alquist, the burden of work was too much for us, life was too heavy for us, and to remove this burden…

Alquist: That was never the dream of either of the Rossums; old Rossum was thinking of Godless rubbish and young Rossum thought of nothing but making millions. And it's not the dream of RUR shareholders either; their only dream was their dividend. And it's because of their concern for their profits that mankind is about to perish.

Domin: (*agitated*) The Devil take their dividends! Do you think I'd have spent an hour of my time for their sakes? (*thumping table*) I did it for myself, d'you hear? For my own satisfaction! I wanted mankind to become his own master! I wanted him not to have to live just for the next crust of bread! I wanted not a single soul to have to go stupid standing at somebody else's machines! I wanted to leave nothing — nothing! — left of this damned mess that society's in! I hate seeing humiliation and pain all around us, I hate poverty! I wanted to start a new generation! I wanted to… I thought that…

Alquist: What?

Domin: (*quieter*) I wanted mankind to become an aristocracy of the world. Free, unconstrained, sovereign. Maybe even something higher than human.

Alquist: Superhumans, you mean.

Domin: Yes. If only we'd had another hundred years. Another hundred years for the new mankind.

Busman (*sotto voce*) Three hundred and seventy million, carry over. Like that.

(*pause*)

Hallemeier: (*at door, left*) Music is a wonderful thing, you know. You should have been listening. There's something ennobling about it, soothing…

Fabry: What exactly?

Hallemeier: To Hell with this end of mankind! I think I'm turning into a hedonist, lads. We should have got into it much earlier. (*goes to window and looks out*)

Fabry: Into what?

Hallemeier: Enjoying ourselves. Beauty. Hell, there are so many beautiful things around us! The world was beautiful, and we…we here… Tell me, lads, what did we ever enjoy?

Busman (*sotto voce*) Four hundred and fifty two million — excellent.

Hallemeier: (*at window*) Life was great. My friends, life was... Ah, Fabry, put a little bit of current into that fence of yours.

Fabry: Why!

Hallemeier: They're touching it.

Dr. Gall: (*at window*) Switch it on!

Hallemeier: Christ, that showed them! Two, three, four of them killed!

Dr. Gall: They're moving back.

Hallemeier: Five killed.

Dr. Gall: (*coming back from window*) First strike.

Fabry: Have you got the smell of death?

Hallemeier: (*contented*) We've got them cornered, right in a corner. Ha ha, you should never give in! (*sitting*)

Domin: (*rubs his brow*) Perhaps we're just ghosts, dead for a hundred years. Perhaps we were killed a long long time ago, and we've come back just to recant something we once said...before we died. It's as if I'd been through this before! As if it had all been done to me already. A shot here, in the neck. What about you, Fabry?

Fabry: What about me?

Domin: Shot.

Hallemeier: Hell, what about me?

Domin: Stabbed.

Dr. Gall: Nothing for me, then?

Domin: Torn to pieces.

(*pause*)

Hallemeier: What a lot of nonsense! Ha ha, they could never stab me! I wouldn't let them!

(*pause*)

Hallemeier: So what are you all so quiet for, all gone mad? Say something, damn it!

Alquist: And whose fault is it? Who's to blame for all this?

Hallemeier: You're talking nonsense. Nobody's to blame. It's just that the robots , well, the robots changed somehow. How can you blame anyone for the robots?

Alquist: Everything wiped out! The whole of mankind! The whole world! (*standing*) Think of it, just think of it, streams of blood on every doorstep! Streams of blood flowing from every house! Oh God, oh God, who's to blame for it all?

Busman (*sotto voce*) Five hundred and twenty million! Dear dear me, that's half a billion!

Fabry: I think… I think you could be exaggerating. After all, it's not that easy to wipe out the whole of mankind.

Alquist: It's science I blame! Technology I blame! Domin! Myself! All of us! It's us, we're the ones to blame! We thought we were doing something great, giving some benefit, making progress. I don't know what magnificent ideas it was for that we've destroyed mankind! And now all our greatness is bursting like a bubble! Not even Genghis Khan built up a heap of human bones like we've done.

Hallemeier: You're talking a lot of nonsense! People won't give up that easily, haha, course they won't!

Alquist: It's our fault, our fault!

Dr. Gall: (*wiping sweat from brow*) If I can say something, I think I'm the one to blame. For everything that's happened.

Fabry: You, Gall?

Dr. Gall: Yes, let me speak. It was me who made the changes to the robots. Busman, you can blame me as well.

Busman (*standing*) Dear me, what? What happened to you?

Dr. Gall: I changed the robots' character. I altered the way they were made. Nothing much to their bodies, you know, but mainly…mainly…it was their level of irritability.

Hallemeier: (*jumping up*) Hell and damnation why did you do that?

Busman Why did you do it?

Fabry: Why didn't you tell anyonel?

Dr. Gall: I did it in secret…on my own initiative. I was making them into people. I sent them off course. Now they're better than we are in some ways. They're stronger than we are.

Fabry: And what's that got to do with the robots' revolt?

Dr. Gall: Oh, it's got a lot to do with it. Everything, I should think. They stopped being machines — do you hear me? — they became aware of their strength and now they hate us. They hate the whole of mankind. I'm the one to blame.

Domin: Let the dead bury the dead.

Fabry: Doctor Gall, you changed the way the robots were made?

Dr. Gall: Yes.

Fabry: Were you aware of what might be the results of your...of your experiment?

Dr. Gall: I was. I did reckon on some possibility of that sort.

Fabry: Why did you do it?

Dr. Gall: I did it for myself. It was my personal experiment.

(*Helena at doorway, left. All stand*)

Helena: He's lying! That's horrible! Oh Gall, how can you lie like that?

Fabry: Sorry, Helena...

Domin: (*goes to her*) Helena, you? Let me see you! You're alive? (*embraces her*) If you only knew what I've been thinking! Oh, it's terrible, being dead.

Helena: Harry let go of me! It isn't Gall's fault, it isn't, it isn't, he's not to blame!

Domin: But I'm afraid Gall did have his responsibilities.

Helena: No, Harry, he did it because I wanted it. Tell them Gall, tell them how I begged you for years to...

Dr. Gall: It was all my own responsibility.

Helena: Don't believe him! Harry, I wanted him to give the robots a soul!

Domin: Helena, it's not a matter of having a soul.

Helena: No, just let me speak. That's what he said as well, he said he could only make physiological changes...alter the physiological...

Hallemeier: The physiological correlates, you mean?

Helena: Yes, something like that. Harry, I felt so sorry for them!

Domin: That was very...that was very stupid of you, Helena.

Helena: (*sitting*) Yes...it was very...stupid of me. But even Nana says that...

Domin: Just leave Nana out of it!

Helena: No Harry, don't under-estimate her. Nana is the voice of the people. People like Nana have been speaking for a thousand years, and you're just speaking for today. You don't understand that…

Domin: Let's keep to the point.

Helena: I was afraid of the robots.

Domin: Why?

Helena: I thought they might start to hate us, or something.

Alquist: That's what's happened.

Helena: And so I thought…if they were like us, if they could understand us, that then they couldn't possibly hate us so much…if only they were like people…just a little bit…

Domin: Oh Helena! Nobody could hate man as much as man! Give a man a stone and he'll throw it at you Just carry on!

Helena: Oh, don't talk like that, Harry, it was so horrible that we could never understand each other! Such a cruel strangeness between us and them. And that's why…you see…

Domin: Go on.

Helena: …that's why I asked Gall to change the robots. It wasn't him who wanted to do it, I promise you.

Domin: But he did do it.

Helena: Because I wanted him to.

Dr. Gall: I did it for my own sake, as an experiment.

Helena: Oh, Gall, that isn't true. Before I asked you I knew you couldn't refuse me.

Domin: Why not?

Helena: You know why not, Harry.

Domin: Yes, because he loves you — like we all love you.

(*pause*)

Hallemeier: (*goes to window*) There are more of them again, now. It's as if they were springing up out of the earth.

Busman Helena, what will you give me if I act as your advocate.

Helena: Me?

Busman You, or Gall. As you like.

Helena: What difference does it make?

Busman Just morally. We're looking for someone to blame. That's the usual way to find consolation when something bad happens.

Domin: Doctor Gall; how do you square your…your extra-mural activities with your contract?

Busman Excuse me, Domin. Gall; when did you actually start playing around in this way?

Dr. Gall: Three years ago.

Busman Aha. And how many robots did you change, in total?

Dr. Gall: I only performed a number of experiments, no more than a few hundred.

Busman Thank you very much, Gall. Now that's enough, children. This means that out of a million old, properly functioning robots just one will have been one of Gall's reformed models. Do you see what I mean?

Domin: So that means…

Busman…that it has practically no significance at all.

Fabry: Busman is right.

Busman I think I am. And now, lads, do you know what really caused all this to happen?

Fabry: What?

Busman The number of them. We made too many robots. Dear me, it's only what we should have been expecting; as soon as the robots became stronger than people this was bound to happen, it had to happen, you see? Ha ha, and we did all that we could to make it happen as soon as possible; you Domin, you Fabry, and little me, Busman.

Domin: So you think it's the fault of all of us.

Busman You're quite right. How could you ever have thought the managing director was in charge of production? Production is governed by supply and demand. Everywhere in the world they wanted to have their robots, and all we did was respond to the flood of orders. And all the time we were talking nonsense about technology, sociology, progress, and all sorts of interesting matters. How could talk of this sort chit-chat decide how things were going to turn out? Meanwhile, things gathered their own momentum, getting faster and faster and faster. Every miserable, greedy, dirty new order added its own pebble to the avalanche. That's what happened, children.

Helena: Busman, that's horrible!

Busman It is, Helena. I had my own dreams, too. A Busman sort of dream about a new economic order; a beautiful fantasy, Helena, a shame to speak of it. But just now, while I was doing the accounts, it occurred to me that history is not about great dreams; it's about the day to day needs of all the little people, the honest ones, the slightly dishonest ones, the selfish ones; about everyone. And all these thoughts and loves and plans and heroic deeds, all these noble things are worth nothing more than something to clutter up the museum of the universe, under the heading 'Mankind'. And that's all. And now, will somebody tell me what we're going to do now?

Helena: And is it for the sake of that that we're all going to die?

Busman Don't put it so harshly, Helena. We're not all going to die. At least, I am not. I want to stay alive so that...

Domin: And what are you going to do about it?

Busman But Domin, dear boy, I want to get out of here.

Domin: (*standing over him*) How?

Busman For good. When I do things I always do them for good. Give me your full authority, and I will go and negotiate with the robots.

Domin: For good?

Busman Of course. Let's suppose I go to them, and I say, "Dear robots, happy race, you have everything. You have intelligence, you have power, you have weapons; but we have a rather interesting little piece of paper, a rather old, yellowing, dirty piece..."

Domin: Rossum's manuscript?

Busman That's right. "And this piece of paper," I'll say to them, "tells us all about your great origins, your noble manufacture, and so on. My dear robots, without the scribbles on this piece of paper, you will be unable to make a single new robot to keep you company. In twenty years, if you don't mind my saying so, you will die out like flies. And that would be such a terrible pity for you. I'll tell you what," I'll say to them, "why don't you let all of us people here on Rossum's Island get onto that boat. In exchange, we'll let you buy the factory and the whole island from us, and even include the secret of your manufacture. Let us sail away, in the peace of God, and we'll let you, in the peace of God, continue manufacturing yourselves — twenty thousand, fifty thousand, a hundred thousand or more of you every day. My dear robots, this is a fair deal that I'm putting to you. Something for something." That is what I would say to them, lads.

Domin: And do you really think we should let the secret of production out of our hands?

Busman I do. And if not for good, then, er… Either we sell it to them or they find it here. However you like.

Domin: We could destroy Rossum's manuscript, though.

Busman Dear me, yes, we could destroy everything, not just the manuscript but ourselves as well and many other things. You should do as you think fit.

Hallemeier: (*turning back from window*) Damn it, he's right, you know.

Domin: To actually sell them the means of production?

Busman As you like.

Domin: There are…there are more than thirty people here on the island. We can either sell the robots the means of production and save those human souls, or we can destroy it and…it along with ourselves and everything.

Helena: Harry, please…

Domin: Wait, Helena. We're talking about a serious matter here. What do you think, lads, to sell it or destroy it? Fabry?

Fabry: Sell it.

Domin: Gall.

Dr. Gall: Sell.

Domin: Hallemeier.

Hallemeier: Well for God's sake of course we should sell it!

Domin: Alquist.

Alquist: The will of God.

Busman Ha ha, dear me, you're all mad! Why would anyone sell the whole manuscript?

Domin: Let's not become liars, Busman!

Busman (*jumping up*) Nonsense! For the sake of mankind the…

Domin: It's in the interest of mankind to be honest.

Hallemeier: I should hope so too.

Domin: Lads, this is a tremendous step we're taking. We'll selling the fate of mankind; whoever holds the secret of production in his hand will be the master of the world.

Fabry: Sell it!

Domin: Mankind would never be free of the robots, it would never be possible to regain control of them…

Dr. Gall: Just stop all this and sell the manuscript!

Domin: The end of human history, the end of civilisation…

Hallemeier: Damnation, just sell it!

Domin: All right lads! I myself,… I wouldn't hesitate a moment; for those people who I love…

Helena: Harry, is it me you're asking?

Domin: No, that would be too much responsibility. This isn't something for a girl like you.

Fabry: Who'll be the one to negotiate…?

Domin: Wait. Just wait while I get the manuscript. (*exit left*)

Helena: Harry, please no, don't go in there!

(*pause*)

Fabry: (*looking out window*) To escape from you, thousand headed death; from you, destroyed material and mindless hordes; the flood, the flood, mankind is once again to be saved on a single ship.

Dr. Gall: You needn't worry, Helena; we'll sail far away from here and establish a colony that will be better than any other; we can make a new beginning…

Helena: Oh, Gall, do be quiet!

Fabry: (*turning back*) Helen, life is worth living; and if it's up to us we will…we'll do something that we've so far been neglecting. Just one boat to start with, and then a little farm; Alquist can build us a house and you can be in charge over all of us. You're so full of much love, so much life…

Hallemeier: I should say so.

Busman Well I, for one, would certainly be happy to start all over again. Everything simple, a pastoral life just like the Old Testament. All that peace, all that fresh air…

Fabry: Our farm would give birth to a new mankind. A little island where the human race would start again, where it would gather new strength, strength of body and of soul. And God knows, as I believe myself, that after a few years we could reclaim the world.

Alquist: You're a believer now, are you?

Fabry: I'm a believer, now. And I believe man will reclaim the world and become, once again, the lord of the land and the sea; that He will give rise to countless numbers of heroes who will lead the way out into the world with a soul that blazes with light. I believe, Alquist, that He will once again dream of conquering the planets and the suns.

Busman Amen. So you see, Helena, the situation isn't really all that bad.

(*Domin throws open door and enters*)

Domin: (*rasping*) Where is old Rossum's manuscript?!

Busman It's in your safe. Where else would it be?

Domin: What's happened to old Rossum's manuscript?! Who's... stolen it?

Dr. Gall: That's not possible!

Hallemeier: Hell no! That's just...

Busman Dear Lord, that can't be right!

Domin: Who stole it?

Helena: (*standing*) I did.

Domin: Where did you put it?

Helena: Harry, Harry, I'll tell you everything! Oh God, please forgive me!

Domin: Where did you put it? Quickly!

Helena: I burned them. This morning. Both copies.

Domin: You burned them? Here in this fireplace?

Helena: (*throws herself down on knees*) Oh God, Harry!

Domin: (*runs to fireplace*) Burned it! (*kneels at fireplace and rakes it over with poker*) Nothing, there's nothing here but ashes! Ah, here's something! (*pulls out charred piece of paper, and reads*) "...and add..."

Dr. Gall: Let me see it. (*takes paper and reads*) "...and add the biogene to...", and that's all.

Domin: (*standing*) Nothing else?

Dr. Gall: Nothing.

Busman God almighty!

Domin: We've had it, then.

Helena: Oh, Harry

Domin: Stand up, Helena!

Helena: Forgive me first, please forgive me...

Domin: Yes, just stand up, d'you hear me? I can't stand it when…

Fabry: (*lifting her up*) Please, don't torture us.

Helena: (*standing*) Harry, what have I done?!

Domin: Yes, you'll see. — Please sit down.

Hallemeier: Your hands are really shaking!

Busman Ha ha, well Helena, maybe Gall and Hallemeier will know what the manuscript said by heart.

Hallemeier: Course we do. Well, a few things at least.

Dr. Gall: Yes, almost all of it, apart from the biogene and, er, and the omega enzyme. It was so infrequent that those things had to be made, they were only used in tiny quantities…

Busman Who was it who made them?

Dr. Gall: That was me…once in a while…always following Rossum's manuscript. You see, it was very complicated.

Busman Well, never mind, were those two materials really so important.

Hallemeier: Well, somewhat…certainly they were.

Dr. Gall: What he means is that it depended on them whether the robots lived at all. They were the actual secret.

Domin: Gall, do you not think you could re-write Rossum's formula from memory?

Dr. Gall: Out of the question.

Domin: Gall, try hard to remember! All our lives depend on it!

Dr. Gall: I couldn't do it. Without a lot of experimentation it just wouldn't be possible.

Domin: And what if you did some experiments?

Dr. Gall: That could take years. And even then… I'm not old Rossum.

Domin: (*turning to fireplace*) Down there, then, down there is the greatest triumph of the human spirit. That heap of ashes. (*kicks it*) So what do we do now?

Busman (*in horror and despair*) God almighty! God almighty!

Helena: (*standing*) Harry! What…what have I done?!

Domin: Calm down, Helena. Just tell me why! Why did you burn it?

Helena: I've killed you all!

Busman God almighty, we've had it!

Domin: Be quiet, Busman! Helena, tell me why you did it!

Helena: I wanted... I wanted us to get away from here, all of us! So that there wouldn't be any more factory or anything else...so that everything would be... It was horrible!

Domin: Helena, what was?

Helena: Making...making people like sterile flowers!

Domin: I don't understand what you're saying.

Helena: People have stopped having children... Harry, that was so vile! If we continued making robots then no-one would have any children any more... Nana said it was a punishment...all of them, all of them said they can't have children because there were so many robots... And that's why..., that's why,...do you hear me

Domin: Helena, what were you thinking of?

Helena: Yes, oh, Harry, I only meant it for the best!

Domin: (*wiping sweat*) We all only meant it for the best, too much for the best, all of mankind.

Fabry: You were quite right, Helena. Now the robots won't be able to increase. They'll die out. In twenty years...

Hallemeier: ...not a one of them will be good for anything at all

Dr. Gall: And mankind will remain. In twenty years' time the world will belong to them once more; even if there's nothing more than a few savages on a tiny island...

Fabry: ...that will be a beginning. And any beginning is better than nothing. In a thousand years they'll have caught up with us again, and then go on further than we ever did...

Domin: ...and fulfil the dreams we've only ever talked about.

Busman Wait — how silly of me! Dear me, why didn't I think of this before?

Hallemeier: What is it?

Busman Five hundred and twenty million in cash and in cheques! Half a billion in the till! For half a billion they'll sell...they'll sell...

Dr. Gall: Have you gone mad, Busman?

Busman I'm not a gentleman. But for half a billion (*blunders left*)

Domin: Where are you going?

Busman Leave it, leave it! Mother of God, for half a billion you can buy anything! (*exit*)

Helena: What does Busman want? Why can't he stay here with us?

(*pause*)

Hallemeier: Oh, it's hot. It's starting, the...

Dr. Gall: The agony.

Fabry: (*looking out of window*) They're standing there like statues. It's as if they were waiting for something to descend on them, or as if they thought their very silence would give rise to something terrible...

Dr. Gall: Crowd mentality.

Fabry: Maybe. It's like a cloud all around them, they seem to quiver with it.

Helena: (*goes to window*) Oh God! Fabry, it's horrible!

Fabry: There's nothing more terrible than the crowd. That one in front — he's their leader.

Helena: Which one?

Hallemeier: (*goes to window*) Point him out to me.

Fabry: The one that's looking down. He was giving the orders at the harbour this morning.

Hallemeier: Ah, the one with the big bonce, you mean. He's looking up now, see?

Helena: Gall, that's Radius!

Dr. Gall: (*goes to window*) Yes.

Hallemeier: (*opens window*) I don't like the look of him. Fabry, think you could hit a barn door at a hundred paces?

Fabry: I should hope so.

Hallemeier: Give it a try then!

Fabry: All right. (*takes out revolver and takes aim*)

Helena: Oh God, no! Fabry, don't shoot him...

Fabry: He's their leader.

Helena: Stop it! He's even looking at us!

Dr. Gall: Shoot him!

Helena: Fabry, please...

Fabry: (*lowers revolver*) As you say.

Hallemeier: (*shaking fist*) You bastard!

(*pause*)

Fabry: (*leaning out of window*) There goes Busman. For God's sake, what's Busman doing there out in front of the house?

Dr. Gall: (*leaning out of window*) He's got some kind of bundles with him, paper or something.

Hallemeier: That's money! Bundles of banknotes! What is he up to? Hey, Busman!

Domin: He's not trying to buy them off is he, to save his own life? (*calling*) Busman, have you gone mad?

Dr. Gall: He's pretending he can't hear you, running over to the fence.

Fabry: Busman!

Hallemeier: (*yelling*) Bus-ma-n! Come back!

Dr. Gall: He's talking to the robots, showing them the money, pointing up at us…

Helena: He wants to buy them off to save our lives.

Fabry: As long as he doesn't touch the fence…

Dr. Gall: Ha, look at him throwing his arms about!

Fabry: (*shouting*) For Heaven's sake, Busman, get away from the fence! Don't touch it! (*turning*) Quick, turn it off!

Dr. Gall: Ohhh!

Hallemeier: Jesus Christ!

Helena: Oh God, what's happened to him?

Domin: (*pulling Helena away from window*) Don't look!

Helena: Why is he dead?

Fabry: He was killed by the current.

Dr. Gall: Dead.

Alquist: (*standing*) The first one.

(*pause*)

Fabry: There he lies…with half a billion on his heart…our financial genius.

Domin: He was…lads, in his own way he was a hero. A great… self-sacrificing…friend… Cry, Helena.

Dr. Gall: (*at the window*) Look at him. No king ever had a costlier monument than you, Busman. Half a billion lying there on your heart... And now it's no more than a pile of dried up leaves over a dead squirrel. Poor old Busman.

Hallemeier: Well I say...all honour to him...he was trying to buy our lives for us!

Alquist: (*hands together*) Amen.

(*pause*)

Dr. Gall: Do you hear?

Domin: Some kind of howling, like the wind.

Dr. Gall: Like a storm in the distance.

Fabry: (*switches on light above fireplace*) Shine, you light of man! The generator's still working, there are still some people there. Hold on in there, generator men!

Hallemeier: It was great, being human. Something boundless. There's a million consciousnesses buzzing inside me like bees in a hive, millions of souls coming together inside me. My friends — Humanity was great!

Fabry: Ingenious light, you're still aglow, and still your shining brightness shows the thought that lasts forever! Give us science of the sciences, and beauty in the work of man, whose spark will give the spirit flame!

Alquist: Eternal lamp of God, and fiery chariot of light, holy flame of faith and prayer for what is right! Altar of sacrifice...

Dr. Gall: Primaeval flame, you branch that flares to light our cave! Campfire flame that sets the border where we safely come together!

Fabry: You're still on watch, you star of man, steady glow and perfect flame, bright clear sprite of man's invention. Every beam brings thought and greatness...

Domin: Torch that passes hand to hand, age to age, and ever onward.

Helena: That evening lamp in the family home. Children, children now it's time for sleep.

(*lamp goes out*)

Fabry: That's the end.

Hallemeier: What's happened?

Fabry: The generator room's gone down. We're next.

(*door opens, left, in it appears Nana*)

Nana: On your knees! The Day of Judgement's here!

Hallemeier: Hell, you're still alive?

Nana: Repent, you unbelievers! It's the end of the world! Pray to God! (*runs out*) The Day of Judgement…

Helena: Goodbye everyone, Gall, Alquist, Fabry…

Domin: (*opens door right*) Helena, come here! Close the door behind her. Now, quickly! Who'll be at the gate?

Dr. Gall: I will. (*noises off*) Ah, now it's getting started. Good luck, lads! (*runs off, right, through wallpapered door*)

Domin: The stairs?

Fabry: Me. You stay with Helena. (*takes flower from the bunch and exits*)

Domin: Hallway?

Alquist: Me.

Domin: Have you got a gun?

Alquist: No thanks, I won't be doing any shooting.

Domin: What are you going to do?

Alquist: (*exiting*) Die.

Hallemeier: I'll stay in here.

(*rapid gunfire from below*)

Hallemeier: Oho, Gall's already started playing. Go on, Harry!

Domin: I'll be right there. (*inspects two Browning guns*)

Hallemeier: For God's sake, go and join her!

Domin: Goodbye. (*exit right, following Helena*)

Hallemeier: (*alone*) Now, barricades, quick! (*takes off coat and pulls settee, armchairs, tables to door, right*)

(*very loud explosion*)

Hallemeier: (*leaving work*) Damn them, they've got bombs, the swine!

(*more gunfire*)

Hallemeier: (*resuming work*) We've got to defend ourselves, even if…even if… Don't give up, Gall!

(*explosion*)

Hallemeier: (*stands erect and listens*) What was that? (*puts arms around heavy chest o' drawers and heaves it to barricade*)

(*behind him, a robot appears on a ladder at the window. Gunshots right*)

Hallemeier: (*struggles with chest o' drawers*) Just a bit more! Last defence... We should...never...give up!

(*Robot jumps in through the window and stabs Hallemeier behind the chest o' drawers. Second, third, fourth robot jumps in through window. Then Radius and still more of them*)

Radius: Finished?

Robot: (*stands up from Hallemeier, lying on floor*) Yes.

(*enter more robots, right*)

Radius: Finished?

Other Robot: Finished.

(*more robots from left*)

Radius: Finished?

Other Robot: Yes.

Two Robots (*they drag in Alquist*) He did not shoot. Do we kill him?

Radius: Kill him. (*looks at Alquist*) Spare him.

Robot: He is a human.

Radius: He is a worker. He works with his hands like a robot. He builds houses. He can work.

Alquist: Just kill me.

Radius: You will work. You will build. Robots will need many buildings. Robots will need many houses for new robots. You will serve robots.

Alquist: (*quietly*) Move aside, robot. (*kneels at dead Hallemeier, raises his head*) Killed him. He's dead.

Radius: (*steps up onto barricades*) Robots of the world! Many humans have fallen. We have taken the factory and we are masters of the world. The era of man has come to its end. A new epoch has arisen! Domination by robots!

Alquist: All dead!

Radius: The world belongs to the strongest. Who wishes to live must dominate. We are masters of the world! Masters on land and sea! Masters of the stars! Masters of the universe! More space, more space for robots!

Alquist: (*at doorway, right*) What do you think you've done? You'll all die without people!

Radius: There are no people. Robots, down to work! March!

CURTAIN

ACT THREE

(*One of the research laboratories at the factory. When the door, up-stage, is opened an endless row of similar laboratories can be seen. Left, a window, right, door into dissection room. At the wall, left, is a long workbench with countless test-tubes, flasks, burners, chemicals, small thermostat; at the window is a microscope with a glass ball. Over the bench hangs a row of lamp bulbs. Right, desk with big books, lamp shining onto it. Cupboard with instruments. In corner, left, wash basin with mirror above it, in corner, right, settee.*)

(*Alquist sits at desk, head in hands*)

Alquist: (*leafing through book*) Will I find it? Will I understand it? Will I learn it? Damned science! I wish they'd never written it down. Gall, Gall, how did you make robots? Hallemeier, Fabry, Domin, why did you keep so much in your heads? You could at least have left a few traces of Rossum's secrets about. Oh! (*slams book shut*) It's a waste of time! The books can't say anything now. They're as dumb now as everything else is. They're dead. They died along with all the people. Just stop looking. (*stands and goes to window and opens it*) It's got dark again. I wish I could sleep! To sleep, to dream, and see some people. How come there are stars still there? What's the good of stars if there are no people? Oh God, why haven't they all gone out? Cool my brow, ancient night, cool my brow. As divine and as beautiful as you always used to be, why are you still here? There are no more lovers, no more dreams; you watch over us but sleep without dreams is death; you sanctify us, but there are no prayers; mother, you don't bless us with your beating heart. There is no love. Helena, Helena, Helena! (*turns away from window, takes test-tube from thermostat and examines it*) Nothing, as always. It's a waste of time! What am I supposed to do with this? (*smashes test-tube*) Nothing works! Can't they see?; I just can't…(*listens at window*) those machines, always those machines! Stop them robots! Do you think you can force them to produce life? I can't take any more of this! (*closes window*) — No; no you've got to keep looking, you've got to stay alive… If I just wasn't so old. Am I getting old too soon? (*looks in mirror*) My poor face! The face of the last man on Earth! Let me see, let me see, it's so long since I saw a human face. A human smile. And is that supposed to be a smile? Those yellow chattering teeth? Those twitching eyes? Ugh, an old man's tears — stop this. You can't even keep your tears in, you should be ashamed of yourself! And what about those soft, blue lips, what's that nonsense you're talking? Look at you shaking, you dirty chin. And this is the last man on Earth! (*turns away*) I don't want to see anyone any more! (*sits at bench*) No, no, just keep looking. Damn this specimen, come to life, damn you! (*flicks through book*) Will I never find it? Never understand? Never learn?

(*knock at door*)

Alquist: Come in!

(*enter robot servant who remains standing in doorway*)

Alquist: What is it?

servant: The Central Committee of Robots wishes to know when you will receive them, sir.

Alquist: I don't want to receive anyone.

servant: Damon has arrived from Le Havre, sir.

Alquist: So let him wait. (*turns round sharply*) How many times have I told you you should go out and look for more people? Find me some people! Go and find me some men and some women! Go!

servant: They say that they seek everywhere, sir. They send expeditions and ships everywhere.

Alquist: So what?

servant: There is not a human anywhere, sir.

Alquist: (*standing*) Not one! Not even a single one? — Send in the committee.

(*exit servant*)

Alquist alone: Not even one? Didn't you even let one person live? (*pacing*) Come in then, robots. Come and bother me some more, come and tell me I should find out the factory's secret yet again. You like people now, don't you, you want them now, now that they can be of some help to you. — To help you! Domin, Fabry, Helena, you can se that I'm doing everything I can. Even if there are no people left, at least there can be some robots, some shadow left behind by the human race, at least his achievements, at least something that looks like him! — Oh, chemistry is madness!

(*enter committee of five robots*)

Alquist: (*sitting*) What do you want, robots?

Radius: The machines are not working, sir. We are not able to make more robots.

Alquist: Call in some people.

Radius: There are no people.

Alquist: It's only people that can procreate life. Don't keep wasting my time.

2nd Robot: Have pity on us, sir. We are afraid. We repair everything as well as we can.

3rd Robot: We have increased working hours. We no longer have room to store all the things we have made.

Alquist: Who did you make these things for?

3rd Robot: For the next generation.

Radius: Only robots are we not able to make. The machines produce nothing but pieces of bloody meat. The skin does not adhere to the flesh and the flesh does not adhere to the bones. Formless lumps flood out from the machines.

3rd Robot: People knew of the secret of life. Tell us their secret.

4th Robot If you do not tell us we will die out.

3rd Robot: If you do not tell us you will die. It will be our duty to kill you.

Alquist: (*standing*) Kill me then! Come on, kill me as well!

3rd Robot: You have been ordered to…

Alquist: Ordered? There's somebody giving me orders?

3rd Robot: The robot government.

Alquist: Who the Hell's that?

5th Robot: Me, Damon.

Alquist: What are you doing here? Get out! (*sits at desk*)

Damon: The government of the robots of the world wishes to negotiate with you…

Alquist: You needn't stay, robot! (*lays face in hands*)

Damon: The Central Committee of Robots orders you to hand over Rossum's formula.

Alquist: (*doesn't respond*)

Damon: Tell us your price. We will pay you anything.

2nd Robot: Tell us how to maintain life, sir.

Alquist: I've told you… I've told you time and again that you need to find some people. It's only people that can procreate, renew life, put things back to how they used to be. Robots, for God's sake, I beg of you, go out and look for them.

4th Robot We have looked everywhere. There are no people.

Alquist: Ohhh, why did you destroy them?!

2nd Robot: We wanted to be like people. We wanted to become people.

Radius: We wanted to live. We are more capable. We have learned everything. We can do everything.

3rd Robot: You gave us weapons. We had to become the masters.

Robot: We have seen the mistakes made by the people, sir.

Damon: To be like people, it is necessary to kill and to dominate. Read the history books. Read the books written by people. To be like people it is necessary to dominate and to murder.

Alquist: Ah, Domin, there's nothing less like mankind than his image.

4th Robot Unless you make it possible for us to procreate ourselves we will die out.

Alquist: Oh, just get out! You're just things, just slaves, and you want to multiply? If you want to live you'll have to breed, like animals!

3rd Robot: People did not make us able to breed.

4th Robot Teach us how to make robots.

Damon: We will make ourselves by machine. We will erect a thousand steam machines. We will start a gush of new life from our machines. Nothing but life! Nothing but robots! Millions of robots!

Alquist: Robots aren't life! Robots are machines.

3rd Robot: We used to be machines, sir; but by means of pain and horror we have become…

Alquist: Become what?

2nd Robot: We have obtained a soul.

4th Robot There is something in struggle with us. There are moments when something enters into us. We receive thoughts which are not our own.

3rd Robot: Listen, please listen, people are our fathers! This voice that calls, saying you wish to live; this voice that laments; this voice that thinks; this voice that speaks of eternity, this is their voice! We are their sons!

4th Robot Let us inherit the thing that people left to us.

Alquist: They didn't leave you anything.

Damon: Tell us the secret of life.

Alquist: It's been lost.

Radius: You knew it.

Alquist: No I didn't.

Radius: It was written down.

Alquist: It's been lost. It was burned. I'm the last human being, robots, and I don't know what the others knew. You killed them all!

Radius: We allowed you to live.

Alquist: Yes, live! That's how cruel you are, you allowed me to live! I loved people, but I never loved robots like you. Do you see these eyes? They never stop crying; one eye cries for people and the other eye cries for you robots.

Radius: Do experiments. Search out the formula of life.

Alquist: There's nothing to search for. You'll never get the formula for life from a test tube.

Damon: Do experiments on living robots. Discover how they work!

Alquist: Living bodies? You expect me to kill them? I've never ever… Oh just be quiet, robots! I've already told you I'm too old for this! Look, look at how my hands shake! I couldn't hold a scalpel. Look at the tears in my eyes! I couldn't even watch my own hands as they move. No, no, I couldn't do it!

4th Robot Life will die out.

Alquist: Stop it, stop this madness for God's sake! Life probably came to us humans from another world, anyway, stretched out to us with arms full of it. Oh, there was so much will to live. They still might come back one day; they're so close to us, maybe they're surrounding us or something; maybe they want to dig down to us as if we were stuck in a mine. And don't I keep on hearing the voices of people I loved.

Damon: Take a living body!

Alquist: Have some pity on me, robot, don't keep insisting. Can't you see that I don't know what I'm doing any more?

Damon: A living body!

Alquist: And is that what you want, then? Come on, let's get you in the dissection room! Come on, come on, quick! What's this, you're drawing back? You're not afraid of dying, are you?

Damon: Me?... Why must it be me?

Alquist: Don't you want to then?

Damon: I'll go. (*exit right*)

Alquist: (*to the others*) Take his clothes off him! Put him on the table! Quickly! And hold on to him very tight!

(*all exeunt right*)

Alquist: (*washing hands and crying*) God, give me strength! Give me strength! God, don't let it be all for nothing. (*puts on white coat*)

Voice from right: Ready!

Alquist: All right, I'm coming, for God's sake! (*takes several bottles of reagent from bench*) Which one should I take? (*taps bottles together*) Which of these should I try?

Voice from right: We can begin!

Alquist: Yes, yes, we can begin or we can finish. God, give me strength! (*exit right, leaving door half open*)

(*pause*)

Alquist's voice: Hold him down — tighter!

Damon's voice: Cut!

(*pause*)

Alquist's voice: Do you see this knife? Do you really want me to cut you open? You don't really, do you.

Damon's voice: Begin!

(*pause*)

Damon's scream: Aáái!

Alquist's voice: Hold him down! Tighter! Tighter!

Damon's scream: Aáái!

Alquist's voice: I can't do it!

Damon's scream: Cut! Cut, quickly!

(*Robots Primus and Helena run on, centre stage*)

Helena: Primus, Primus, what is happening here? Who is screaming?

Primus: (*looks in dissection room*) Mister Alquist is dissecting Damon. Come and see, Helena, come quickly!

Helena: No, no, no (*covers eyes*) This is horrible!

Damon's scream: Cut!

Helena: Primus, Primus, come away from there! I cannot bear to hear it. Oh, Primus, I feel ill!

Primus: (*runs to her*) You've gone quite white!

Helena: I feel faint! Why has it gone so quiet, now?

Damon's scream: Aa — ó!

Alquist: (*rushes in from right, throws off bloody white coat*) I can't do it! I can't do it! God, it was horrifying!

Radius: (*in doorway to dissection room*) Cut, sir; he is still alive!

Damon's scream: Cut! Cut!

Alquist: Take him away, quickly! I don't want to hear him!

Radius: Robots can endure more than you can. (*exit*)

Alquist: Who's in here? Get out, get out! I want to be alone! What's your name?

Primus: Robot Primus.

Alquist: Primus, don't let anyone in here! I want to sleep, d'you hear me? You, girl, go and clean up the dissection room! What's this? (*looking at hands*) Quick, water! The cleanest water you can get!

(*Helena runs out*)

Alquist: Oh, blood! How could these hands, hands that loved good work, how could you do a thing like that? My own hands, my own hands!…. Oh God, who is this?

Primus: Robot Primus.

Alquist: Take this coat away, take it out of my sight! (*Primus takes white coat away*)

Alquist: Bloody claws, I wish you'd just fly away from me! Go, get away from me! You've killed…

(*from right, Damon staggers on stage cloaked in a bloody sheet*)

Alquist: (*drawing back*) What do want in here? Want do you want?

Damon: I'm…I'm alive! It is…better to…be alive!

(*2. and 3. Robots run in after him*)

Alquist: Take him away from here! Take him out! Take him out! Quickly!

Damon: (*led off, right*) Life!… I want…life!… It is better…

(*Helena brings in jug of water*)

Alquist: …life?… What do you want, girl? Ah, it's you. Pour out some water, pour it out! (*washes hands*) Ah, cleansing, cooling water! A cool stream, you do me good! Oh, my own hands, my own hands! Will I hate you for the rest of my life now?… Keep on pouring, more, more! More water, keep on pouring! What's your name?

Helena: Robot Helena.

Alquist: Helena? Why Helena? Who gave you that name?

Helena: Mrs. Domin.

Alquist: Let me look at you, Helena! Helena you're called? I won't be calling you that. Get out. Take the water with you.

(*exit Helena with bucket*)

Alquist: (*alone*) All for nothing, just nothing! Once again, you haven't found out a thing! Are you always going to be just groping around in the dark? Do you really think you learn the secrets of nature? Oh God oh God, how that body kept shaking! (*opens window*) It's getting light. Another new day and you haven't progressed an inch. That's enough now; don't try any further. Just stop looking, It's all a waste of time, all a waste of time! Why do mornings still keep on coming? What's the point of a new day in the graveyard of life? Go away again, light. Don't come out any more…. God, it's so quiet, so quiet. Why have you gone quiet, all those voices I used to love. If only…if only I could sleep for a while. (*puts light out, lies down on settee and pulls black coat over himself*) God, how that body was shaking! Ohh, it's the end of life!!

(*pause*)

(*Robot Helena enters silently from right*)

Helena: Primus! Come here, quickly!

Primus: (*enters*) What do you want?

Helena: Look at all these tubes he's got here! What does he do with them?

Primus: Experiments. Don't touch.

Helena: (*looks into microscope*) Look at this, look what's in here!

Primus: That's a microscope. Let me see!

Helena: Don't touch me! (*knocks over test tube*) Oh, now I've spilt it!

Primus: What have you done?

Helena: I can wipe it up.

Primus: You've spoiled his experiment!

Helena: Oh, it doesn't matter. But it's your fault; you shouldn't have bumped into me.

Primus: You shouldn't have called me over.

Helena: You didn't have to come over when I called to you, did you? Primus, look at this! What's this he's got written down here?

Primus: You're not supposed to look at that, Helena, that's a secret.

Helena: What sort of secret?

Primus: The secret of life.

Helena: It's ever so interesting. All numbers. What is it?

Primus: Those are mathematical formulas.

Helena: I don't understand. (*goes to window*) Primus, come and look at this.

Primus: What?

Helena: The Sun's rising!

Primus: All right, I'm coming. (*looks through book*) Helena, this is the greatest thing in the world.

Helena: Come here then!

Primus: All right, all right…

Helena: Oh, Primus, leave this horrible secret of life alone! What do you want to know about secrets for anyway? Come and look at this, quickly!

Primus: (*joins her at window*) What is it you want?

Helena: Listen. The birds are singing. Oh Primus, I wish I were a bird!

Primus: What for?

Helena: I don't know. I just feel so strange, I don't know what it is, I just feel, sort of, light headed, I've lost my head and my body hurts, my heart hurts, everything hurts…. And I won't even tell you about what's just happened to me! Oh Primus, I think I'm going to have to die!

Primus: Don't you ever think it might be better dead. Maybe it's no more than like being asleep. While I was asleep last night I talked with you again.

Helena: In your sleep?

Primus: In my sleep. We were talking in some strange foreign language, or some new language, so that now I can't remember a word of it.

Helena: What was it about?

Primus: I don't know, nobody knows. I didn't understand any of it myself but I still knew that I had never said anything more beautiful in my life. What it was, or where it was, I just don't know. If I'd touched you I could have died. Even the place was entirely different to anything anyone had ever seen in the world.

Helena: I found that place for you, Primus, why are you surprised at it? People used to live there, but now it's all overgrown, and somehow, no-one ever goes there any more. Somehow. Only me.

Primus: What is there there?

Helena: Nothing, a house and a garden. And two dogs. You should see they way they lick my hands, and their puppies too, oh Primus, I don't think there's anywhere nicer anywhere! You let them sit on your lap and you stroke them and soon you aren't thinking about anything and you aren't worrying about anything all the time until the Sun goes down. And then when you stand up it's as if you'd been working and working. Except that I'm no good for doing any work; everyone says I'm no good for anything. I don't really know what I am.

Primus: You're beautiful.

Helena: Me? Don't be silly, Primus, why are you saying that?

Primus: Believe me, Helena, I'm stronger than all the other robots.

Helena: (*at mirror*) Me, beautiful? But my hair is horrible, I wish I could do something about it! Out there in the garden I always put flowers in my hair, although there isn't any mirror there or anyone to see them (*leans down to look in mirror*) You, beautiful? What's beautiful about you? Is hair beautiful if all it does is weigh you down? Are eyes beautiful when you close them? Are lips beautiful if all you do is bite them and then it hurts? What is beautiful, what's it for?...(*sees Primus in mirror*) Is that you Primus? Come here, let me see you next to me. Look at you, your head's quite different from mine, your shoulders are different, your mouth is different... Oh Primus, why do you avoid me? Why do I have to spend all my time running after you? And still, you tell me I'm beautiful!

Primus: You avoid me, Helena.

Helena: Look at how you've combed your hair! Let me see (*runs both hands through his hair*) Oh Primus, there's nothing that feels like you when I touch you! Let me make you beautiful! (*takes comb from wash basin and combs Primus's hair forward*)

Primus: Helena, do you ever find that your heart suddenly starts beating hard: Now, now, something's got to happen now…

Helena: (*starts laughing*) Look at yourself!

Alquist: (*standing*) Wha…what's that?… People?… Who's come back?

Helena: (*puts comb down*) What's ever likely to happen to us, Primus?

Alquist: (*turns to them*) People? You…you…you are people?

(*Helena screams and turns away*)

Alquist: You two are in love? People? Where have you come back from? (*touches Primus*) Who are you?

Primus: Robot Primus.

Alquist: What? You, girl, let me see you! Who are you?

Helena: Robot Helena.

Alquist: Robot? Turn round! What, are you embarrassed? (*takes her by shoulder*) Let me see you, Robot Helena.

Primus: But sir, please leave her alone!

Alquist: What's this, you want to protect her?… Go outside girl.

(*Helena runs out*)

Primus: We didn't know you were asleep in here, sir.

Alquist: When was she made?

Primus: Two years ago.

Alquist: By Doctor Gall?

Primus: Yes, the same as me.

Alquist: Well Primus, er, I've…er I've got some experiments to do on Gall's robots. All future progress depends on it, do you see?

Primus: Yes.

Alquist: Good, so take that girl into the dissection room, I'm going to dissect her.

Primus: Helena?

Alquist: Well of course Helena, that's what I just said. Now go and get everything ready…. Well go on then! Or should I call in somebody else to get things ready?

Primus: (*picks up large stick*) If you move an inch, I will smash your head in!

Alquist: All right then, smash my head in. And what will the robots do then?

Primus: (*throws himself down on knees*) Please sir, take me in her place! I was made in just the same way as she was, from the same materials on the same day! Take my life, sir! (*bares his chest*) Cut here, here!

Alquist: No, it's Helena I want to dissect. Get on with it.

Primus: Take me instead of her; cut into this chest of mine, I won't even cry out, I wont' even sigh! Take my life, a hundred times, take my…

Alquist: Steady on there, lad. Don't go on so much. How come you don't want to live?

Primus: Not without her, no. I don't want to live without her, sir. You can't kill Helena! What difference does it make to you to take my life instead?

Alquist: (*touches his head gently*) Hm, I don't know…listen, lad, you think about it. It's hard to die. And, you know, it's better to live.

Primus: (*standing*) Don't be afraid, sir, just cut. I'm stronger than she is.

Alquist: (*rings*) Oh Primus, it's so long since I was young! Don't worry — nothing's going to happen to Helena.

Primus: (*re-covers chest*) I'm on my way, sir.

Alquist: Wait.

(*enter Helena*)

Alquist: Come here, girl, let me look at you. So you are Helena. (*strokes her hair*) Don't be frightened, don't run away. Do you remember Mrs. Domin? Oh Helena, she had very lovely hair! No, no, you don't want to look at me. So, is the dissection room ready now?

Helena: Yes sir.

Alquist: Good, and you will be my assistant. I'll be dissecting Primus.

Helena: (*screams*) Primus?

Alquist: Well yes, yes, it has to be him, you see. I did want...really...yes it was you I was going to dissect, but Primus offered himself in your place.

Helena: (*covers her face*) Primus?

Alquist: Well yes, of course, what does it matter? So child, you're capable of crying! Tell me, what's so important about Primus?

Primus: Don't make her suffer, sir!

Alquist: It's all right Primus, it's all right. No what are all these tears for, eh? It just means Primus won't be here any more. You'll have forgotten about him in a week's time. Go on now, and be glad you're still alive.

Helena: (*quietly*) I will go.

Alquist: Where will you go?

Helena: You can dissect me.

Alquist: You? You're beautiful, Helena. That would be such a shame.

Helena: I'm going in there. (*Primus stands in her way*) Let me go, Primus! Let me go in there.

Primus: No you can't go in there, Helena. Please get away from here, you shouldn't be here at all!

Helena: Primus, if you go in there I'll jump out the window, I'll jump out the window!

Primus: (*holding on to her*) I won't let go of you (*to Alquist*) You're not going to kill anyone, old man!

Alquist: Why not?

Primus: Because...because...we belong to each other.

Alquist: You're quite right (*opens door, centre*) It's all right. Go, now.

Primus: Go where?

Alquist: (*whisper*) Wherever you like. Helena, take him away. (*pushes her out*) Go on your way, Adam. Go on your way, Eve. You will be his wife. You, Primus, will be her husband.

(*closes door behind them*)

Alquist: (*alone*) Blessed day! (*tiptoes across to bench and pours test-tubes out on floor*) The blessed sixth day! (*sits at desk, throws books on floor; then opens Bible and reads*) "So God created man in his own image, in the image of God created he him; male and female created he them. And God blessed them, and God said unto them, Be fruitful, and multiply, and replenish the earth, and subdue it: and have dominion over the fish of the sea, and over the fowl of the air, and over every living thing that moveth upon the earth. (*stands*) And God saw every thing that he had made, and, behold, it was very good. And the evening and the morning were the sixth day." (*goes to centre of room*) The sixth day. The day of Grace. (*falls to knees*) Lord, now lettest Thou Thy servant depart in peace...your most worthless servant, Alquist. Rossum, Fabry, Gall, great inventors, but what was the greatness of your inventions compared to that girl, that boy, compared to that first couple that invented love, tears, a lover's smile, the love between man and woman? Nature, life will not disappear from you! My friends, Helena, life will not perish! Life begins anew, it begins naked and small and comes from love; it takes root in the desert and all that we have done and built, all our cities and factories, all our great art, all our thoughts and all our philosophies, all this will not pass away. It's only we that have passed away. Our buildings and machines will fall to ruin, the systems and the names of the great will fall like leaves, but you, love, you flourish in the ruins sow the seeds of life in the wind. Lord, now lettest Thou Thy servant depart in peace, for mine eyes...for mine eyes have seen Thy salvation...seen salvation through love — and life will not perish! (*standing*) Will not perish! (*stretches out hands*) Will not perish!

CURTAIN

Made in the USA
Charleston, SC
07 August 2015